QUILTS AND AFGHANS
from McCall's Needlework and Crafts

QUILTS & AFGHANS

from
McCall's
Needlework & Crafts

SEDGEWOOD™ PRESS
NEW YORK

For Sedgewood™ Press
Editorial Director, Sedgewood™ Press: *Jane Ross*
Project Directors: *Marilyn Pelo*
                     Cynthia Vartan
Managing Editor: *Gale Kremer*
Designer: *H. Roberts*
Production Manager: *Bill Rose*

Distributed in the Trade by Van Nostrand Reinhold

ISBN 0-442-28202-8
Library Of Congress Catalog Number 83-51236

Manufactured in the United States of America

CONTENTS

INTRODUCTION

HOMEMADE QUILTS AND AFGHANS have more in common than their shared function: keeping people warm. They are both living forms of folk art, awe-inspiring examples of the ingenuity and native artistic talents of American women.

Quilt making is perhaps the most American of all needlecrafts, one of our original art forms and a part of our heritage. Initially inspired by necessity, it evolved into a means of individual artistic expression, an opportunity to illustrate and preserve family traditions and important events in American life. Eventually eclipsed by mass-produced substitutes, homemade quilts began to enjoy a rebirth of appreciation in the 1960s when the back-to-basics movement embraced the freshness and originality of handmade crafts. In recreating traditional patchwork or appliqué patterns, legions of modern needleworkers are rediscovering the treasure trove that American women created from their imaginations and the contents of their scrap bags.

In Part I of this book, "Quilts," you will find several of the most popular patchwork patterns and examples of other traditional styles as well. But there are also imaginative personal interpretations of classic designs and some quilts with a more contemporary look, including several appliqué patterns particularly suitable for children's rooms. The quilts chosen for this collection are representative of the best of the new and the old, illustrating the craft's diversity and continuing vitality.

In Part II, "Afghans," diversity is again the key with a kaleidoscope of patterns to suit every taste and setting. As creative activities and forms of self-expression, knitting and crocheting have enjoyed enduring appeal to both young and old, and of all the popular knitting and crocheting projects, afghans have long been at the top of the list. The reasons are easy to understand. Afghans can be made quickly and easily. They are economical, often using scraps of yarn left over from other projects. An afghan can put a personal stamp on any room, and it makes a practical and appreciated present for almost any occasion.

Presented here are patterns for both the beginner and for the more experienced crocheter and knitter: patterns with origins rooted in the past, modern interpretations of old-fashioned patterns and contemporary picture designs. In addition, the group of crocheted afghans includes both designs crocheted in and cross-stitched on afghan stitch.

All quilt and afghan projects are accompanied by explicit step-by-step instructions, many clear patterns and diagrams, and full-color photographs, all carefully designed to help you create something uniquely your own as easily and pleasurably as possible.

P A R T I

QUILTS

Traditional patterns. Contemporary looks. Amish styles. Designs for children. Modern interpretations. The quilts that follow reflect a spectrum of patterns, from the old favorite patchwork Bear Paw to a Country Christmas wall hanging; from the elegant Fan, reminiscent of "crazy" quilts, to the abstract geometrics of the Amish Diamond; from Heirloom's twenty traditional appliqué patterns to that best friend of generations of children, Sunbonnet Sue. The choice is up to you.

Seminole Stripes Quilt

Inspired by Seminole Indian patchwork, this brilliant-hued, banner-like quilt is made up of seven panels—six of them pieced—plus a border, all of which can be machine-pieced and machine-quilted. It will add a bold stroke of color to any space.

SIZE: 82¼″ × 58¼″.

EQUIPMENT: Pencil. Ruler. Scissors. Thin, stiff cardboard. Tailor's chalk.

MATERIALS: Closely woven cotton (or cotton blend) fabric, 45″ wide: navy, 2½ yards; orange-red, 1¼ yards; hunter green, ½ yard; light orange, ½ yard. Fabric for lining, 45″

wide, 3⅛ yards. Dark orange sewing thread. Thin layer of batting or other thin filler such as a summer blanket.

DIRECTIONS: Read General Directions on pages 97–102. Quilt is made up of seven panels (six of them pieced), plus border. It may be pieced and quilted on the machine.

Sawtoothed Panels: To make pattern, mark a 9½" square on cardboard. Draw a diagonal line between two corners. Cut on marked lines for triangle pattern. Marking pattern on wrong side of fabric and adding ¼" seam allowance all around, cut eight triangles each from orange-red and green fabrics. Make eight pieced squares by sewing orange-red and green triangles together on their long sides. Sew pieced squares into two panels of four squares each, keeping triangles always in the same alternating position.

Striped Panels: Cut two strips each 2" × 38" from navy, orange-red, green, and light orange fabrics, adding ¼" seam allowance all around. Sew strips together on their long sides to make two panels, using one strip of each color for each panel; sew stripes in order of colors listed.

Birds-in-Flight Panels: Make a triangle pattern as before, using a rectangle 3¾" × 4⅝". Cut patch pieces as before, 32 each of navy and light orange. Make 32 pieced rectangles, joining navy and light orange triangles on their long sides. Join two pieced rectangles on their 4⅝" navy sides to make a larger rectangle; make 16 large rectangles. Join large rectangles on their long sides to make two panels of eight rectangles each, keeping apex of large navy triangles always pointed in the same direction.

To complete panels, cut four pieces ½" × 7½" from orange-red fabric, adding ¼" seam allowance all around. Sew an orange-red piece to each end of panels.

Center Panel: From orange-red fabric, cut piece 12" × 38", adding ¼" seam allowance all around.

Assembling: Join all seven panels on their long sides for main body of quilt in following order: sawtoothed, striped, birds-in-flight, center, birds-in-flight, striped, and sawtoothed; reverse order of the triangles panels in second half of quilt (see color photograph). Piece should measure 38" × 62", plus outside seam allowance.

Border: From navy fabric, cut four pieces 9½" wide, two 38" long and two 81" long, adding ¼" seam allowance all around. Sew shorter pieces to top and bottom of quilt, then longer pieces to sides. Piece should measure 57½" × 81½", including outside seam allowance.

Lining: Cut two pieces 41¼" × 57½". Sew together on long sides with ½" seams; press seam open. Cut lightweight batting (or other filler) same size.

Quilting: Following general quilting directions on pages 100–101, pin and baste quilt top, batting, and lining together. Mark quilting lines with ruler and tailor's chalk, placing quilt vertically as shown in illustration. Dividing orange-red center panel into thirds, mark two horizontal lines in center of panel 4" apart. On top and bottom navy borders, mark horizontal line 3" from green triangles, then another line 3" from first line. Mark same pattern on long side borders.

Use dark orange thread for all quilting (or a shade that will show up on both the light orange and orange-red fabrics). Starting in the center and working outward in both directions, quilt on marked lines; quilt also close to long seams of orange-red center panel and light orange and orange-red stripes; quilt close to two inner seams of light orange and orange-red triangles. Quilt around main body (pieced center) of quilt, extending stitching line on long sides out to edge of navy border.

FINISHING: From orange-red fabric, cut four pieces 1¾" wide, two 81½" long and two 59¼" long, piecing to get lengths. Placing right sides together and making ¼" seams, sew longer pieces to sides of quilt, then shorter pieces to top and bottom. Turn under outside edge of pieces ¼", turn to back of quilt, and slip-stitch folded edge along seam line, making ⅝" edging around quilt.

Fan Quilt

This innovative design is a beautiful combination of a traditional quilt pattern executed with the elegance of Victorian "crazy" quilts. Silk-like dress fabrics in dazzling colors create the fan, lustrous green moiré completes the square, and delicate embroidery laces each rib. As a bonus, there is a charming pillow to match.

Fan Quilt

SIZE: 81¾″ × 93½″.

EQUIPMENT: Pencil. Graph paper. Tracing paper. Large (10″) compass. Ruler. Yardstick. Thin, stiff cardboard. Glue. Scissors. Sewing and embroidery needles. Protractor (optional). Iron. Tailor's chalk. Large safety pins. Quilting hoop or frame (optional).

MATERIALS: Moiré taffeta, 44" wide, 5 yards dark green, 2⅔ yards off-white. Scraps of medium-weight, silk-like dress fabrics (such as satin, faille, brocade, moiré taffeta, shantung, polished cotton) in a variety of solid colors, totalling about 4-5 yards. Dark green, soft cotton fabric, 44" wide, 5¼ yards. Muslin, 48" wide, 2½ yards. Dark green velvet ribbon, ⅜" wide, 13½ yards. Batting. Six-strand embroidery floss in a variety of colors. Sewing and quilting threads, dark green and off-white.

DIRECTIONS: Quilt is made up of 30 pieced and embroidered fan blocks, set with stripping and borders.

Patterns: To cut patch pieces for the blocks, make three templates, referring to diagram: On graph paper, mark a 10¾" square. Set compass for 3¾", place point in lower right corner, and draw an arc, for pattern B. Set compass for 9¾"; place point in same corner and draw an arc; corner area opposite B is pattern C. For A, trace actual-size pattern. Glue papers to cardboard, let dry; then cut on lines drawn for templates. When cutting patches, replace templates as soon as edges begin to fray from repeated use.

Patch Pieces: Place each template on wrong side of designated fabric, with right angles of B and C and one long edge of A on straight of goods. Using sharp pencil held at an outward angle, mark around template. Continue to mark all pieces required of one color, leaving ½" between outlines. When all

pieces are marked, cut out each one ¼" beyond marked lines for seam allowance; the marked lines will be the stitching lines.

From dark green moiré taffeta, cut 30 of piece C; use 2 yards of fabric, reserving remainder for borders. From assorted dress fabrics (see Materials), cut 30 of piece B and 180 of piece A.

Block: From muslin, cut 30 pieces 11¼" square. For each block, sew eight patch pieces to a muslin foundation: Choose six A pieces, a B piece and a C piece; study color photograph for ideas in harmonizing or contrasting colors. Following diagram, baste C piece to corner of

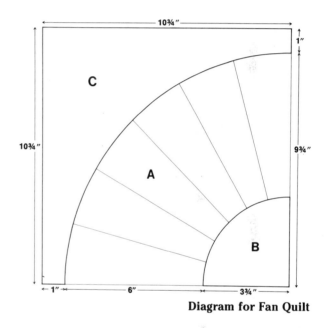

Diagram for Fan Quilt

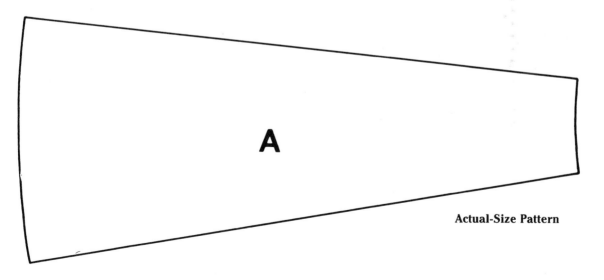

A

Actual-Size Pattern

muslin square, keeping all seam allowances flat and matching outer raw edges.

To aid in placing A pieces, set compass for 10″; place point in B corner (see diagram) and draw an arc on C piece, ¼″ from raw edge of curve. (As a further aid, you can use a protractor to mark five points on arc, making six 15° segments.) On each A piece, fold under seam allowance of longer curved edge and press. Begin sewing on A pieces: Place one A right side up at bottom of block, matching a long raw edge with raw muslin edge and aligning pressed curve edge with marked curve on C; baste in place. Place a second A piece over first, right sides facing, and stitch along inner long edge through all three layers, following marked seamline. Turn second A over to right side and press seam. Add a third A to second in same manner. Add fourth A. If you did not mark off the five points suggested, check accuracy at this time by placing a straight edge diagonally across block to see if seam joining third and fourth A pieces aligns with C and B corners. Add remaining A pieces; the outer raw edge of sixth piece should align with raw edge of muslin. Slip-stitch outer curve of entire A section in place.

Before completing block, add embroidery: Using all six strands of floss in needle, embroider five designs on block, working on or over seams joining A pieces. See page 104 for some of the designs we used, or work out your own. Each design is a combination of several stitches, such as straight stitch, chain, lazy daisy, French knot, herringbone, blanket, feather-stitch, couching, cross-stitch, woven spider web, and cretan stitch, as well as variations of these stitches. (See page 103 for Stitch Details.) Combine colors as desired; we used two, three, or four colors in each design (see photograph).

Turn under seam allowance on curved edge of B piece and press, clipping so piece lies flat. Baste B in place, aligning raw edges; pressed edge of B should overlap A section ¼″. Slip-stitch B to A along curved edge.

Cut 16″ piece of green velvet ribbon. Center and pin over A-C seam; slip-stitch along outer edge, then inner edge.

Make 30 blocks in this manner.

Assembling Quilt Top: From off-white moiré taffeta, cut a piece along the length 20″ wide and set aside for borders. From remaining fabric, cut joining strips 1½″ wide, 24 of them 11¼″ long and five 58¼″ long (measurements include ¼″ seam allowance); cut all strips on lengthwise grain of fabric.

Lay out the 30 quilt blocks into six horizontal rows of five blocks each, arranging colors as desired; in first, third, and fifth rows, place blocks with B piece in lower left corner; in second, fourth, and sixth rows, place B pieces in lower right corner.

Add four 11¼″ joining strips to each row, placing one between every two blocks; stitch long edges of each strip to adjacent blocks, right sides facing and making ¼″ seams; press seam allowance under blocks. Each row should measure 58¼″ long. Place 58¼″ strips between rows and join to rows as for blocks. Quilt top should now measure 58¼″ × 70″, including outside seam allowance. If your piece measures otherwise, adjust length of following border strips accordingly.

Borders: From moiré taffeta, cut three sets of four border strips each: 1) off-white, 2½″ wide, two 62¼″ long and two 74″ long. 2) green, 8¼″ wide, two 77¾″ long and two 89½″ long. 3) off-white, 2½″ wide, two 81¾″ long and two 93½″ long. Join first set to quilt top with ¼″ seams, centering shorter pieces along top and bottom and longer pieces at sides; miter corners. Join second set in same manner, then third set. Quilt top should measure 81¾″ × 93½″.

Lining: From green cotton fabric, cut two pieces 41⅜″ × 93½″. Sew together on long edges with ½″ seam, to make lining same size as quilt top. Cut layer of batting same size.

Quilting: Using yardstick and tailor's chalk, mark three quilting lines 1¹⁵⁄₁₆″ apart, the length of each green border piece; lines will meet at corners.

Place lining flat, wrong side up. Place batting on top; anchor to lining with two long stitches crossing in center. Place quilt top over batting; pin layers together temporarily with large safety pins. Baste generously through all thicknesses: First, baste on the lengthwise and crosswise grain of fabric, then diagonally in both directions and around sides, top and bottom.

If desired, attach quilt to a frame or insert in a quilting hoop. If using neither hoop nor frame, you can quilt in your lap, working over a small area at a time. Using a short, strong needle and strong cotton thread (or quilting thread), begin quilting with running stitch in two separate motions: Push needle straight down through all layers with one hand, take needle with other hand, pull thread through and push up close to first stitch; see detail. Make stitches as small and close as possible; space stitches evenly so they are same size on both sides.

Starting in center of quilt and working around and outward toward edge, quilt on each block along curves, using white thread to quilt on A section close to B, and green thread to quilt on C section close to green ribbon; quilt around each block and around outer edge of first border with white, on marked lines of second border with green, around inner edge of third border with white.

FINISHING: To bind edges, cut 2"-wide strips from green moiré taffeta, two 82¾" long and two 94½" long. Turn under one long edge of each strip ½" and press. Pin strips to front of quilt, with right sides facing and matching raw edges; center strips so that ½" extends at each end. Stitch strips in place with ½" seam. Fold strips to reverse side of quilt, mitering corners; slip-stitch corners and pressed edges in place.

Fan Pillow

SIZE: 16¾" square.

EQUIPMENT: Pencil. Graph paper. Tracing paper. Large (10") compass. Ruler. Thin, stiff cardboard. Glue. Scissors. Sewing and embroidery needles. Iron. Protractor (optional).

MATERIALS: Green moiré taffeta, piece 11¼" square. Scraps of dress fabrics (see Fan Quilt). Muslin, piece 11¼" square. Dark green velvet ribbon, ⅜" wide, 2⅜ yards. Very dark green velveteen, 36" wide, ½ yard. Six-strand acetate embroidery floss in a variety of colors. Sewing thread, dark green and white. Fiberfill.

DIRECTIONS: Piece and embroider one fan block, referring to directions in Fan Quilt for Patterns, Patch Pieces and Block; include ribbon trim.

For pillow, cut two pieces 17¼" square from green velveteen. For pillow top, center fan block on right side of one velveteen piece; stitch in place, ¼" from raw edge of block. From velvet ribbon cut four pieces 17¼" long. Place one piece horizontally across pillow top, centering over an edge of block to cover both seam and raw edge; slip-stitch ribbon in place on both long edges. Cover opposite edge of block in same manner, then the vertical edges, overlapping first two ribbons.

Place pillow front and second green piece together, right sides facing. Stitch around edges, making ½" seam and leaving an opening in one side. Turn pillow cover to right side, stuff fully with fiberfill, and slip-stitch opening closed.

Broken Star Quilt

A variation on the time-honored star theme, this particular quilt was made in Missouri about 1930. Here executed in fire-hot hues, it is entirely pieced—with diamonds for inner and outer star, squares and triangles for the background, stripes for the border.

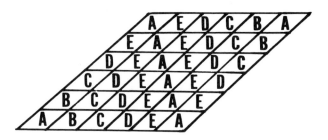

SIZE: About 92″ square.

EQUIPMENT: Ruler. Scissors. Pencil. Thin, stiff cardboard. Tracing paper. Paper for pattern. Dressmaker's carbon (tracing) paper. Tracing wheel or dry ball-point pen. Sewing and quilting needles. Quilting frame (optional).

MATERIALS: Closely woven cotton fabric, 45″ wide: 2⅝* yards each of dark orange (A), light yellow (B), gold (C), light orange (D), and medium orange (E); 3 yards white. Fabric for lining 50″ wide, 5¼ yards. Polyester or cotton batting. White sewing thread.

Note: Less fabric will be required if you wish to piece border strips.

DIRECTIONS: Read General Directions on pages 97–102. Quilt is made up of a "broken" star pieced from diamond patches and set in a white background, bordered with stripes.

Diamond Patches: Trace actual-size pattern; complete quarter-pattern indicated by dash lines for diamond shape. Cut several diamond patterns from cardboard, replacing when edges begin to fray.

Note: Before cutting fabric patches, test accuracy of pattern by drawing around it eight times, to create an eight-pointed star; there should be no gaps or overlapping of diamond segments.

Marking patterns on wrong side of fabric and adding ¼″ seam allowance all around, cut diamond patches as follows: Cut 256 diamonds from dark orange (A), 128 from light yellow (B), 192 from gold (C), 256 from light orange (D), and 320 from medium orange (E).

Joining Diamonds: Center star of quilt is made up of eight identical, pieced, diamond-shaped sections meeting at center point; each section is made up of six rows of six diamond patches each. See Piecing Diagram for one section. Outer portion of large star is made up of 24 more of the same diamond-shaped sections, joined for a circular design. Make 32 diamond-shaped sections as follows.

To make one section, stitch together six rows, following Piecing Diagram and color key; start first row with a dark orange patch

(A), second row with light yellow (B), etc. Use one of the two methods for joining diamonds described in the following paragraph. When joining diamonds to form a row, stitch patches together along sides cut on straight of goods. Stitch from the wide-angled corner toward the pointed ends. Trim seam at points as you piece. Matching corners carefully, join the six rows together to make a diamond-shaped section. When joining rows together, you will be stitching along the bias edges; keep thread just taut enough to prevent seams from stretching. Press pieced sections with seams to one side; open seams tend to weaken construction.

There are two methods for joining the diamonds.

First method: Hold patches together, right sides facing; seam together with small running stitches on pencil lines. If the problem of sharp points and true meeting of seams proves difficult with this method, prepare each patch as follows.

Second method: Cut firm paper patterns the exact size and shape of cardboard pattern. Fit paper pattern within pencil outline on wrong side of patch; hold patch with paper pattern uppermost. Fold seam allowance over each side, and tack to the paper with one stitch on each side, allowing the thread to cross the corners. Finish by taking an extra stitch into the first side; cut the thread, leaving about ¼″. To make removal of tacking easier, do not knot thread or make any backstitches. Hold prepared patches right sides together, matching the edges to be seamed exactly. Whip together with fine, even stitches (about 16 to the inch), avoiding the paper as much as possible. The paper patterns may remain in place until the star shape is completed. To remove the papers, snip tacking thread once on each patch and withdraw thread; lift papers out.

Assembling: For center star, join four sections for each half, with dark orange (A) points meeting in center; join halves for star. Each point of star should measure 12″ (plus outside seam allowance) along side edges.

For background blocks, cut cardboard pattern 12″ square. Marking pattern on wrong side of fabric and adding ¼″ seam allowance all around, cut 20 blocks from white fabric. Cut cardboard pattern in half diagonally for triangle pattern and cut eight triangles from white fabric in same manner.

Sew eight square background blocks to the center star, fitting two sides of a block between two points of star. Sew remaining diamond-shaped pieced sections together in eight groups of three sections each, as if assembling three points of a star. Sew three-pointed sections in the wide angle formed by the square background blocks; sew adjacent sections to each other. Sew remaining 12 square blocks into four corner sections of three blocks each. Sew corner sections and triangle background blocks to star (see illustration). Piece should measure 82″ square, plus outside seam allowance.

Border: Cut four strips 1″ × 84″ from light yellow fabric, adding ¼″ seam allowance all around. Sew a strip to each side of quilt top, with an equal amount extending at each end. Miter corners as follows: Lay piece flat, right side down. Hold adjacent ends together at corners with right sides facing. Keeping border flat, lift up inner corners and pin strips together diagonally from inner corners to outer corners; baste, then stitch on basting line. Cut off excess fabric to make ¼″ seam; press seam open. Cut four 1″-wide strips from remaining colors as follows, adding ¼″ seam allowance all around and sewing on in same manner: gold 86″, light orange 88″, medium orange 90″, and dark orange 92″. Quilt top should measure 92½″ square, including outside seam allowance.

Lining: Cut two pieces 47″ × 93″. Sew together on long sides with ½″ seam; press

seam open. Lining measures 93″ square. Cut batting 92″ square.

Quilting: With ruler and tailor's chalk, mark lines ¼″ and ¾″ in from seams around square blocks, two sides of triangle blocks. Enlarge Feather Quilting Pattern on a paper ruled in 1″ squares. (See Patterns, page 97.) Complete quarter-pattern. Using carbon and a tracing wheel (or dry ball-point pen), transfer pattern to center of square background blocks. Transfer half of pattern to triangle blocks, with half-line of pattern on seam.

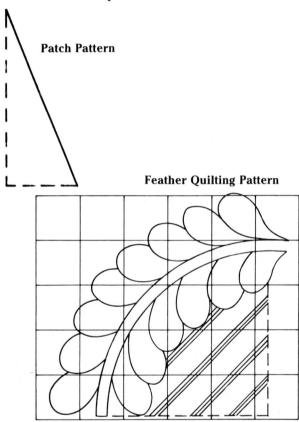

Patch Pattern

Feather Quilting Pattern

Following general quilting directions on pages 100–101, pin and baste quilt top, batting, and lining together, centering layers. Lining extends ½″ all around beyond batting and quilt top extends ¼″. Starting at center and working around and outward, quilt on all marked lines and ¼″ in from all seams of diamond patches and border strips.

FINISHING: Turn excess ½″ of lining over edge of batting and baste in place. Turn in ¼″ seam allowance of quilt top. Slip-stitch folded edges of lining and quilt top together. Press edges.

Heirloom Quilt

A stunning autumn sampler is made up of twenty blocks, each appliquéd with a different design, combined with a flower-and-vine border. Many of the patterns are steeped in American quilting tradition and bear names like Martha Washington Wreath, Prairie Flower, Pennsylvania Tulip, and Ohio Rose.

SIZE: 81″ × 95″.

EQUIPMENT: Pencil. Ruler. Paper for patterns. Tracing paper. Thin, stiff cardboard. Glue. Scissors. Dressmaker's tracing (carbon) paper. Dry ball-point pen. Tailor's chalk. Pins. Large safety pins. Compass. Sewing needle. Embroidery needle.

MATERIALS: Closely woven cotton fabric in small prints, 45″ wide: rust, 2⅝ yards; dark green, 1½ yards; dark brown, gold, and tan, ½ yard each. Unbleached muslin, 81″ wide, 5¼ yards (includes 2⅔ yards lining). Six-strand embroidery floss, green, and brown. White sewing and quilting threads. Batting.

DIRECTIONS: Quilt is made up of 20 blocks, each appliquéd with a different design, plus an appliquéd border (see black and white illustration). Going from top to bottom and from left to right in each row, number each block in illustration.

Blocks: Draw lines across Block Patterns connecting grid lines; there are 17 quarter patterns, two half patterns, and one whole pattern. Heavy lines indicate appliqués; light lines, embroidery; short dash lines, quilting. Enlarge patterns by copying on paper ruled in 1″ squares. (See Patterns, page 97.)

From muslin, cut strip 38″ × 90″; use to cut 20 blocks 12½″ square. On each block mark vertical and horizontal center lines with ruler and tailor's chalk (or crease and press). Place an enlarged pattern on each block, matching dash lines with center lines for one quarter or one half of design as required; there will be a ¼″ margin around outside edge of block. Slipping dressmaker's carbon under pattern, go over general outline of appliqué design only with dry pen, to transfer. Repeat in each quarter or half until complete outline is transferred.

See Appliqué, page 100. Following directions, make cardboard patterns (or templates) for each individual appliqué; trace actual-size hexagon for Block 6 and diamond for Block 14, for greater accuracy. Cut and prepare pieces and hand-appliqué in place following color key for fabrics: From rust, cut strip 11″ × 62″ from lower left side of yardage and use for appliqués, reserving remainder. For Blocks 6 and 14, you may prefer to piece each flower before appliquéing. For Block 18, cut eight 1″-square pieces from rust; fold into quarters and insert into green buds for tips; tack in place, leaving extended points free. For curved strips, stitch inner edge first, then outer edge.

When all appliqué is completed, replace patterns on blocks and transfer embroidery lines. Using three strands of floss in needle, embroider stems and leaf veins in outline stitch with green (use brown for acorns in Block 17). In Block 11, use brown floss to embroider eye in satin stitch and feet in chain stitch. In Block 18, outline gold flowers and centers in brown; add straight stitches around centers. (See page 103 for Stitch Details.)

Joining Blocks: Lay out blocks into five horizontal rows of four blocks each, following illustration or as desired. From rust fabric, cut piece 25″ across width and 32½″ long from upper left corner; use to cut 25 strips 2½″ × 12½″, cutting two across width. Place strips between blocks and at beginning and end of each horizontal row. Join blocks and strips

with ¼″ seams. Rows should measure 58½″ long. Cut six strips 2½″ × 58½″ from left side of rust fabric and join rows as for blocks. Piece should measure 58½″ × 72½″.

Borders: For inner border, cut two pieces 9″ × 58½″ and two pieces 9″ × 89½″ from muslin. Sew shorter pieces to top and bottom of quilt top, then longer pieces to sides, making ¼″ seams. Enlarge Border Patterns and make templates as for blocks. Cut appliqué pieces for 14 flowers, about 150 single leaves, and 14 buds, cutting seven bud tips from rust and seven from gold. For vines, cut long 1″-wide bias strips from green; turn under long edges ¼″ and press, being careful not to stretch fabric. Pin flowers around border as shown. Curve vine strips between flowers and cut to fit, inserting ends under flowers. Pin leaves and buds in place, inserting ends under vines and alternating bud colors. Appliqué border.

For outer border, cut two pieces 4½″ × 81½″ and two pieces 4½″ × 89½″ from rust. Sew longer pieces to sides of quilt top, then shorter pieces to top and bottom, making ¼″ seams. Quilt top will measure 83½″ × 97½″.

Quilting: Transfer quilting lines to blocks. Studying illustration and using compass and tailor's chalk, mark concentric circles about ½″ apart on some blocks, skipping over appliqués. Trace Cable Quilting Pattern and transfer to rust joining strips, repeating across strips lengthwise and widthwise.

Cut lining 81″ × 95″ from muslin. Cut batting same size. Place quilt top flat, wrong side up. Center batting on quilt top with 1¼″ margin all around; secure with large safety pins around edges. Place lining over batting, right side up; pin, then baste through all layers, lengthwise, crosswise, and diagonally. Turn quilt to right side.

Starting in center and working around and outward, quilt on marked lines and around each separate appliqué, using white thread. On blocks with unmarked backgrounds, quilt a line around entire appliqué design, following general contour; continue to quilt separate lines out to edge, following contour; make lines about ¼″ or ½″ apart as desired; study illustration for variations. Quilt on each rust

Border Patterns

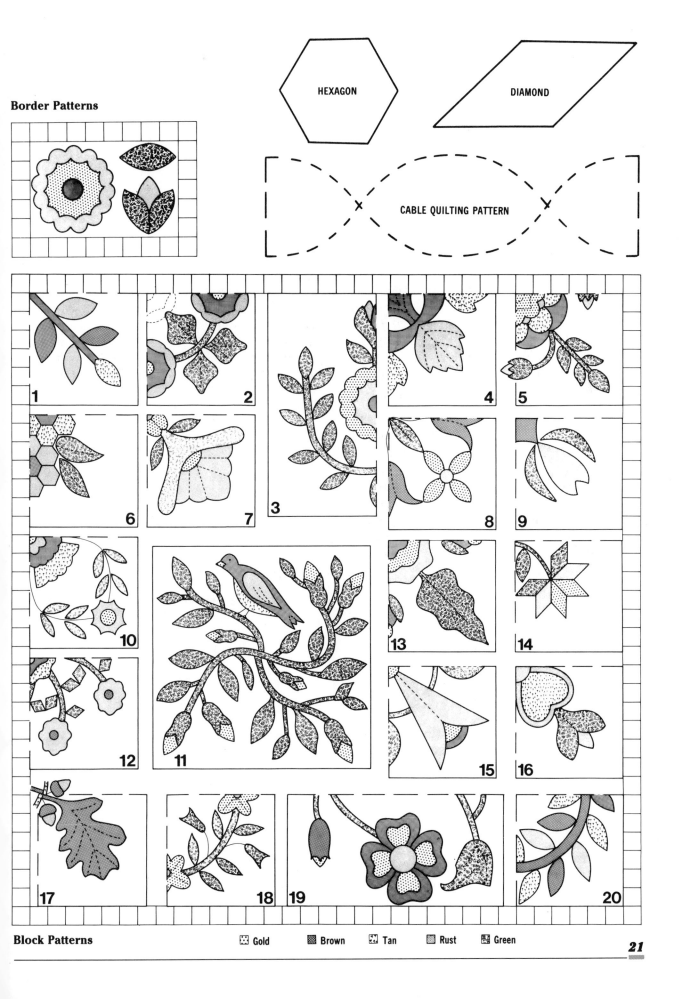

HEXAGON

DIAMOND

CABLE QUILTING PATTERN

Block Patterns

Gold Brown Tan Rust Green

joining strip, 3/16″ in from edges, and around inner edge of white border. Quilt around border appliqués, then around outer edge of white border and inner edge of rust border. (See Quilting Stitch, page 101).

FINISHING: Press edges of rust border 1/4″ to wrong side. Turn excess fabric to wrong side and slip-stitch to lining, making 3″ border on front, 1″ on lining.

Bear Paw Quilt

Hailing from the Amish country of Ohio, this old favorite patchwork pattern often is made with many scraps. But it can have dramatic impact in just two colors—here, black and a strong blue. Nine pieced blocks are set with plain joining strips and borders.

SIZE: 76¾" square.

EQUIPMENT: Pencil. Ruler. Scissors. Thin, stiff cardboard. Paper for patterns. Tracing paper. Tailor's chalk. Dressmaker's (carbon) tracing paper. Tracing wheel (or dry ball-point pen). Sewing and quilting needles. Quilting frame (optional).

MATERIALS: Closely woven cotton fabric, 45" wide: black (with polished finish), 2⅔ yards; bright blue, 2 yards. Fabric for lining, 45" wide, 4⅜ yards. Black sewing thread. Polyester or cotton batting.

DIRECTIONS: Read General Directions on pages 97–102. Quilt is made up of nine pieced blocks, set with plain joining strips and borders.

Patches: Piecing Diagram is one block. Referring to diagram, make cardboard patterns for patch pieces as follows: A—4" square. B—Cut a 2" square in half diagonally for triangle pattern. C—2" × 4". D—2" square.

Marking patterns on wrong side of fabric and adding ¼" seam allowance all around, cut patch pieces as follows: From black fabric, cut 36 of A, 144 of B, and 45 of D. From blue fabric, cut 144 of B, 36 of C, and 36 of D.

Blocks: For each block, join black and blue triangles on their long sides to make 16 pieced squares. Following Piecing Diagram, join the pieced squares with four A pieces, four C pieces, five black D pieces, and four blue D pieces to make one block 14" square, plus outside seam allowance. Make eight more blocks in same manner.

Assembling: From black fabric, cut six pieces 6½" × 14", adding ¼" seam allowance all around. Sew pieced blocks into three rows of three blocks each, with a black piece between rows. Cut two black strips 6½" × 55", adding ¼" seam allowance all around. Assemble the three rows with a black strip between rows, for main body of quilt top. Piece should measure 55" square, plus outside seam allowance.

Borders: From blue fabric, cut four pieces 2¼" wide, two 55" long and two 59½" long; add ¼" seam allowance all around. Sew

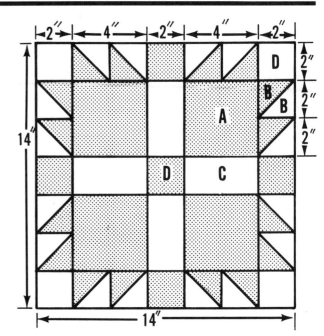

Piecing Diagram

shorter strips to top and bottom of quilt top, then longer strips to sides. Quilt top should now measure 59½" square, plus outside seam allowance.

From black fabric, cut four pieces 8" wide, two 59½" long, and two 75½" long, adding ¼" seam allowance all around. Sew strips to quilt top in same manner as before. Piece should now measure 75½" square, plus outside seam allowance.

Lining: Cut two pieces 38⅞" × 76¾". Sew together on long sides with ½" seams to make lining 76¾" square. Press seam open. Cut batting same size as lining.

Quilting: On each pieced block, mark diagonal lines ⅝" apart with ruler and tailor's chalk; mark lines on all blocks in same direction.

Enlarge Quilting Patterns Nos. 1 and 2 on paper ruled in 1" squares. (See Patterns, page 97.) Using dressmaker's carbon and tracing wheel (or dry ball-point pen), transfer Pattern No. 1 to the two long black strips in main body of quilt top, repeating pattern for the length of strips. Transfer same pattern to the six black pieces between blocks. Transfer Pattern No. 2 to the outside black border, side strips first, then top and bottom.

Insert tailor's chalk in compass; set compass for 1⅛" spread. Draw circles 2½" in

Quilting Pattern 2

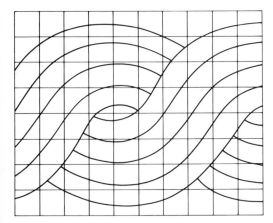

Quilting Pattern 1

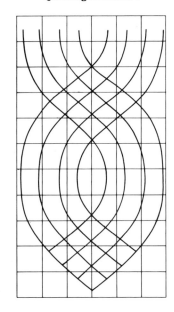

Quilting Diagram

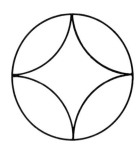

Quilting Pattern 3

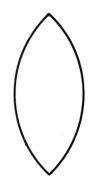

diameter all around blue border. Trace actual-size Quilting Pattern No. 3; make cardboard pattern. Place pattern inside each circle four times and draw around with tailor's chalk, to make design shown in Quilting Diagram.

Following general quilting directions on pages 100–101, center quilt top over batting and lining; pin and baste together. Starting in center and working around and outward, quilt on all marked lines.

FINISHING: From blue fabric, cut four strips 1¾″ × 77¼″. With right sides together and with ¼″ seams, sew strips to front of quilt. Fold strips to back of quilt, turn in raw edges ¼″, and slip-stitch to lining, making a ⅝″ edging on front and back of quilt.

Tulip Quilt

Red and green calico prints are combined in this unusual, stylized tulip design. The festive flowers are appliquéd to 16-inch squares of unbleached muslin, which are then joined in rows of five. Sized for a double bed, it can brighten up any morning.

SIZE: 80″ × 92″.

EQUIPMENT: Ruler. Pencil. Paper for patterns. Thin, stiff cardboard. Scissors. Straight pins. Needles. Light and dark pencils, hard and sharp. Tracing wheel. Dressmaker's carbon paper. Quilting frame (optional).

MATERIALS: Closely woven cotton fabric 36″ wide: small green print, 3 yards; small dark red print, 3 yards. Unbleached muslin, 45″ wide, 5⅓ yards. Matching sewing thread. Cotton batting.

DIRECTIONS: Read General Directions on pages 97–102; read Appliqué on page 100. Enlarge patterns on 1″ squares; complete quarter-patterns indicated by dash lines. For appliqués, make a separate cardboard pattern for each part of appliqué. Cut and prepare appliqué pieces. Cut 25 pointed blocks of dark red print fabric; cut 106 tulip tips and 106 tulip centers (indicated by elliptical shape on tulip pattern) of dark red print fabric; cut 106 tulip cups and stems of green print fabric; cut 106 leaves of green print fabric; reverse pattern and cut 106 more. From unbleached muslin, cut two borders, 6″ × 80″, and 25 squares, 16″ × 16″, adding ¼″ seam allowance all around pieces. Pin, baste, and slip-stitch appliqués in place.

Appliqué the dark red print blocks to centers of each 16″ square with points facing each corner. Following pattern and color

photograph, appliqué one flower motif (tulip, stem, and two leaves) to each corner of pointed block. Appliqué three flower motifs across top border (6″ × 80″ piece), placing one 6″ in from left and right edges, one at center. Do the same across bottom border. Join blocks together (five across and five down); join top and bottom borders, being certain that flower motifs run in same direction. Press seams open.

Quilting: Place quilt top on large flat surface. Using dressmaker's carbon paper, tracing wheel, and quilting motif pattern, mark each square, placing a quilting motif between each flower motif (four quilting motifs to a square).

Cut unbleached muslin lining the same size as quilt top. Pin and baste quilt top, batting, and lining together as directed in general quilting directions on pages 100–101. Quilt along marked quilting lines, using white thread. On remaining areas, including top and bottom borders, work diagonal lines of quilting ⅝″ apart to within ½″ of edges.

FINISHING: When quilting is completed, trim away edges of cotton batting ¼″ all around edge. Turn edges of quilt top over edge of batting. Turn in edges of quilt lining; fold edges of lining over top and stitch all around for finished edge on all four sides of quilt.

Appliqué Patterns

Quilting Pattern

Amish Diamond Quilt

With the elegant simplicity that is the hallmark of Amish design, a simple geometric design is worked in a sophisticated blend of colors, then elaborately finished with several exquisite quilting patterns.

SIZE: About 76" square.

EQUIPMENT: Tracing paper. Paper for patterns. Dressmaker's (carbon) tracing paper. Ruler. Yardstick. Scissors. Pencil. Tracing wheel. Tailor's chalk. Sewing and quilting needles. Straight pins. Large compass or piece of string. Quilting frame (optional).

MATERIALS: Quilt top: Closely woven cotton fabric, such as broadcloth, 44"–45" wide; dark purple, 3 yards; deep turquoise, 1½ yards; bright pink, ⅞ yard; dark maroon, ⅞ yard. Lining: Closely woven cotton fabric, 44"–45" wide, 2¼ yards. Black sewing thread

and threads to match fabrics. Polyester or cotton batting.

DIRECTIONS: Read General Directions on pages 97–102. Mark strips, squares, and triangles on wrong side of fabric, the lengths and widths indicated on Piecing Diagram. Cut out pieces, adding ¼" all around for seam allowance.

Note: Pieces may be cut before beginning construction of the quilt top; however, since seam allowances may vary slightly in the sewing, pieces may also be measured and cut as you progress, for greater accuracy. If this alternate method is selected, be sure to measure accurately each side of the completed square before cutting the adjoining strips. The strips to be joined should be the exact length (including ¼" seam allowance at each end) as the pieces to which they are being joined.

Following Piecing Diagram and starting with center square, begin joining pieces as follows. With right sides together and using marked line as seam line, sew a purple square in place at each end of two of the 3"-wide pink strips. Join these strips to opposite sides of center square. Sew remaining 3" strips in place, completing center square. Press seam allowances flat. Continue adding pieces in this manner until quilt top is complete. Piece should measure 73½" square, with outside seam allowance.

Lining: Cut two strips of lining fabric, each 36¾" × 73½". Sew the two long edges together with ½" seam allowance. Press seam open. Cut batting same size as lining and quilt top.

Quilting: Trace actual-size patterns for Princess Feather and center Star; complete

quarter-pattern of the star indicated by dash lines. Using compass and tailor's chalk, mark two concentric circles in center of center square: outer circle, 19½" in diameter; inner circle, 12½" in diameter.

Note: If large enough compass is not available, the following method may be used: Tie one end of string securely to pencil. Pin other end of string to center of square, leaving 9¼" of string between pencil and pin. Swing pencil around fabric to mark 19½" outer circle. Using same center point and leaving 6¼" of string between pencil and pin, mark 12½" inner circle.

Place center line of Princess Feather motif on each drawn circle. Using dressmaker's carbon and tracing wheel, repeat feather pattern until each circle is complete. Marking with tailor's chalk, divide center of quilt top into eight equal sections; place a diamond in each section for an eight-pointed star. Enlarge remaining quilting patterns on paper ruled in

Princess Feather Pattern

Piecing Diagram

☐ PINK

▦ TURQUOISE

⊠ PURPLE

Schoolhouse Quilt

The nostalgic design of the ever-popular little red schoolhouse is patchwork, graphically pieced together from unbleached muslin and red percale. It's the perfect gift for those going away to school, or those who recall the days when schools really were little and red.

SIZE: 72″ × 91¾″; to lengthen to 107½″, add an extra row of schoolhouses.

EQUIPMENT: Paper for patterns. Pencil. Ruler. Scissors. Stiff, thin cardboard. Straight pins. Sewing needle. Dressmaker's carbon in light (but not white) color. Tracing wheel. Tailor's chalk in light color. Quilting frame (optional).

MATERIALS: Unbleached muslin, 5½ yards, 72″ wide. Red percale, 1¾ yards, 36″ wide. White sewing thread. Cotton batting.

DIRECTIONS: Read General Directions on pages 97–102. Enlarge patterns for schoolhouse and for border quilting motif by copying on paper ruled in 1″ squares; complete half-pattern for quilting motif, indicated by dash lines. Cut all pieces of schoolhouse and background areas indicated by heavy outlines out of cardboard.

For each schoolhouse block, mark outline of cardboard pattern pieces on wrong side of percale and muslin, leaving at least ½″ between pieces. Cut out the 12 red pieces of red percale, and the 11 white pieces of muslin, adding ¼″ on all edges for seam allowances. Use marked lines for stitching lines. With right sides facing, pin edges of all block pieces together; stitch on seam lines. Make 20 schoolhouse blocks in same manner. Cut piece of cardboard 5″ × 9¾″. Mark outline of this piece 16 times on wrong side of muslin, allowing at least ½″ between each. Cut out each piece, adding ¼″ on all edges for seam allowance. Use marked line for stitching line. With right sides facing, pin a muslin piece between top and bottom of each of five schoolhouse blocks to make four vertical strips of five schoolhouse blocks each. Stitch all horizontal seams between the blocks. To join the four vertical strips, cut three strips of muslin each 5½″ × 74¼″ (this includes ¼″ on all edges for seam allowance). With right sides facing, pin schoolhouse strips and muslin strips together; stitch vertical seams.

Borders: At top and bottom of schoolhouse piece are muslin borders. Cut borders 9¾″ × 54½″ of muslin (this includes seam allowance of ¼″ on all edges, except ½″ on one long edge of each, which will be outer top and

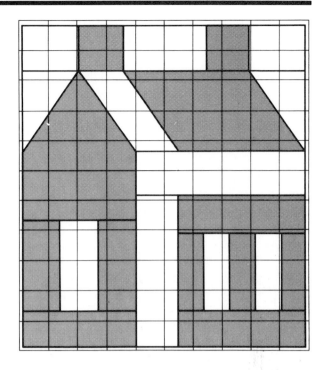

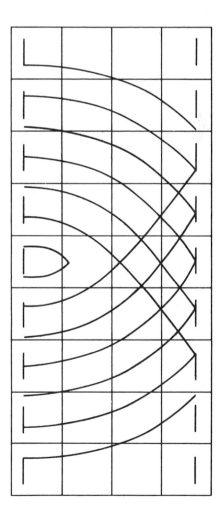

bottom edges). Pin top and bottom borders to quilt with right sides facing; stitch ¼″ seams. Cut two side borders of muslin, each 9¾″ × 92¾″ (this includes seam allowances of ¼″ on inner edge and ½″ on each end and outside edge). Pin borders to sides of quilt, with right sides facing; stitch ¼″ seams.

Lining: For back of quilt, cut one piece of muslin for center 54½″ × 92¾″ (this includes seam allowances of ¼″ at each side and ½″ each at top and bottom edges). Cut side borders as for front sides; pin and sew to quilt back with right sides facing.

Quilting: Mark quilting lines on quilt top with ruler and tailor's chalk. Mark diagonal lines ⅝″ apart on front of all muslin strips and pieces between schoolhouse blocks. Make lines match lines in adjoining pieces and strips. Cross with diagonal lines ⅝″ apart going in opposite direction for diamond

pattern. In each corner, mark a 9½″ square area. Pin curved border pattern on side border immediately below corner, with carbon paper between. Go over tracing with tracing wheel to transfer lines to muslin; continue motif until side is completely marked. Mark other side border and top and bottom borders. In each corner, mark diamond pattern, joining ends of lines to ends of border lines if possible.

Pin and baste quilt top, lining, and batting together as directed in general quilting directions on pages 100–101. First make quilting stitches along all edges of each piece of schoolhouse block (both percale and muslin pieces). With small running stitches, quilt along all lines of diamond pattern and curving lines of the borders.

FINISHING: Turn edges of muslin in ½″ all around quilt and stitch all around twice, 1/16″ and ¼″ in from edges.

Ribbon-Stripe Quilt

This most unusual turn-of-the-century Amish quilt can be made with fabric strips or ribbons—or both. With its easy-to-piece pattern and straight-line quilting, it is an ideal project for beginning quilters.

SIZE: About 78½″ × 79½″.

EQUIPMENT: Ruler. Tailor's chalk. Scissors. Tracing paper. Dressmaker's (carbon) tracing paper. Tracing wheel. Sewing and quilting needles. Straight pins. Sewing machine (optional). Pencil. Quilting frame (optional).

MATERIALS: For stripes, use yard goods, seam binding, or ribbons in seven plain colors, plus one striped and one checked print; see directions for colors and individual amounts. For borders, 36″-wide fabric: ⅔ yard

light navy print, 1 yard dark navy print, scraps of light brown. For lining, 44″–45″ wide fabric, 4½ yards. Navy bias tape, 9 yards. Polyester or cotton batting. White sewing thread.

DIRECTIONS: Read General Directions on pages 97–102. Quilt is constructed of 63 stripes plus side panels and a narrow border with contrasting corners. Cut stripes 1½″ wide × 71½″ long (includes ¼″ seam allowance all around) or cut stripes into random widths (¾″, ⅝″, 1″, 1½″, plus seam allowance) as in original quilt. Piece to get length where necessary. Original quilt has some stripes cut on the bias and some on the straight of fabric. Use either all cut on the straight, or some bias and some straight, but not all bias. Cut 4 aqua stripes, 8 blue, 11 pink, 6 navy, 10 red, 4 tan, 4 light green, 8 green striped, 8 purple checked. Join stripes on long edges, right sides together and with ¼″ seam allowance; stripes can be sewn on the machine, if desired. Starting in center of quilt with pink stripe and working to right, join stripes as follows: purple checked, green striped, navy, aqua, blue, pink, red, tan, red, pink, blue, aqua, navy, green striped, purple checked, red, purple checked, green striped, navy, light green, blue, pink, red, tan, red, pink, blue, light green, purple checked, green striped, pink. Starting from center pink stripe again, join remaining stripes, working to left and repeating design.

For side panels, cut two pieces 5″ × 71½″ from light navy print and sew them to each side of striped center, right sides together and with ¼″ seam allowance. Cut two stripes from tan 1¼″ × 71½″ and sew to side panels in same manner. Cut two stripes 1¼″ × 74″ from blue fabric and sew across top and bottom of quilt top. Cut four 3¼″-wide pieces from dark navy print, two 73″ long and two 74″ long. Sew the 73″ pieces to sides of quilt top. Cut four pieces from light brown fabric 3¼″ square; sew one to each end of 74″ pieces. Sew pieces to top and bottom of quilt top. Quilt top should now measure about 78½″ × 79½″.

Lining: Cut two pieces 40¼″ × 78½″; sew together along long sides, right sides together and with ½″ seam allowance. Press seam open. Cut batting to match quilt top and lining.

Corner Quilting Pattern

Quilting: With ruler and tailor's chalk, mark straight quilting lines on striped center of quilt top and on narrow stripes of border. Mark lines ¼″ from seam lines on each side; on narrow border stripes (and if using some narrow stripes in center of quilt top), mark one line down center. Using dressmaker's carbon and tracing wheel, transfer larger quilting pattern to light navy side panels, repeating design to cover panels. Transfer corner quilting pattern to each corner of border, ½″ from outer sides; repeat single cable design from inside of larger pattern across each border.

Pin and baste quilt top, batting, and lining together, following general quilting directions on pages 100–101. Quilt on all marked lines.

FINISHING: Insert edges of quilt into fold of bias tape and sew edges of tape to top and lining of quilt. Press all around.

Larger Quilting Pattern

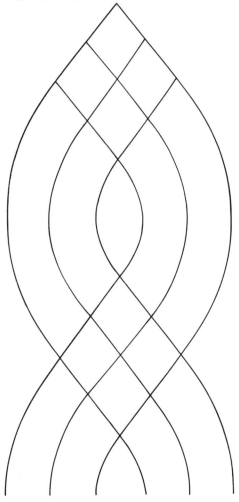

Pine Tree Quilt

The forest has never seemed as friendly and inviting as it does in this design. First, patch a tree in a square, then assemble on the diagonal for a wall hanging that brings year-round cheer to any room. The finished quilt is just the right size for a twin bed.

SIZE: About 55″ × 70¾″.

EQUIPMENT: Pencil. Ruler. Graph paper, 8 squares to the inch. Glue. Thin, stiff cardboard. Scissors. Sewing and quilting needles. Yardstick. Tailor's chalk. Iron. Quilting frame (optional).

MATERIALS: Closely woven cotton fabric, 44″ wide, 4 yards white, 2½ yards dark green, 2 yards print, 2 yards bright red. Fabric for lining, 36″ wide, 4 yards. Matching sewing threads. White quilting thread. Polyester batting.

DIRECTIONS: Quilt is made up of 32 pieced blocks, plus plain and pieced borders.

Patterns: To make templates for pieced blocks, mark patterns on graph paper with ruler and sharp pencil and label as follows, referring to diagrams for Blocks I, II, III. Each triangle pattern is a right-angle triangle, made by bisecting a square from corner to opposite corner; dimension is given for side of the square. Glue graph paper to cardboard; let dry; then cut on marked lines as directed for template. Pattern A—1″ square. B—1″ triangle. C—4″ triangle. D—1¾″ × 6⅝″ rectangle. E—2⅝″ triangle. F—mark 5⅜″ square; mark 1⅜″ triangle in upper left corner and 4″ triangle in upper right corner; cut away triangles for five-sided figure. G—mark 3″ × 5″ rectangle; mark 3″ triangle at one end and cut away for four-sided figure. H—5″ triangle. I—mark 2″ × 9″ rectangle; mark 2″ triangle at one end and cut away for four-sided figure. J—mark 2″ × 11″ rectangle; mark 2″ triangle at one end and cut away for four-sided figure. K—3½″ triangle. L—mark 2″ × 11″ rectangle; mark 2″ triangle at both ends, leaving long sides 7″ and 11″; cut away triangles for four-sided figure.

Patch Pieces: To cut patch pieces, place template on wrong side of fabric, with right angle (for piece L, parallel edges) on straight of goods; mark around with sharp pencil held at an outward angle. Mark as many pieces as needed of one color at a time, leaving ½″ between pieces. Cut out pieces ¼″ beyond marked line, which will be stitching line. From white fabric, cut 54 of A, 684 of B, 18 of E, 36 of F, 36 of G, 10 of I, 10 of J, and 4 of L. For

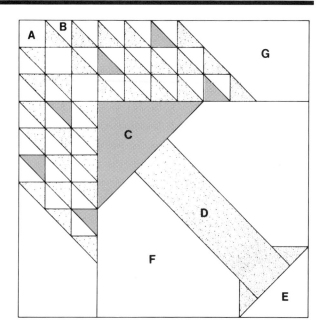

following pieces, cut along length of goods on one side, leaving other side uncut for borders. From green fabric, cut 672 of B, 1 of C, 18 of D, 10 of H, and 4 of K. From print fabric, cut 102 of B and 17 of C. From red fabric, cut 14 of A and 26 of B.

Blocks: To join pieces for blocks, place two adjacent pieces together, right sides facing, and stitch on marked line for ¼″ seam. Press seam to one side, under darker color. In each block, begin by sewing B triangles into B squares, being careful not to stretch bias edges, then sewing A and B squares together in rows, following block diagrams. Sew rows to each other and to larger units of block.

Make 17 of Block I, using green, white, and print pieces. Make another Block I, substituting red for the print B pieces and green for the print C piece. Blocks should measure 11½″ square, including outside seam allowance. Make 10 of Block II and four of Block III, using green, white, and red pieces. Blocks should measure 11½″ and 8¼″ on right angle sides, respectively.

Assembling: Arrange the 32 blocks as shown in color illustration, then sew together in diagonal rows with ¼″ seams; sew rows together for complete design. Piece should measure about 47¼″ × 63″, including outside seam allowance. Measure your piece and adjust border dimensions if necessary.

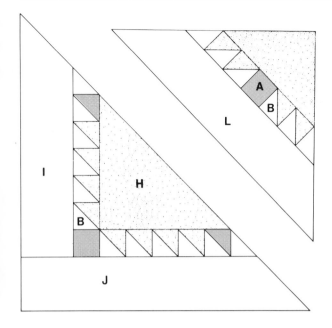

Note: We have altered Blocks II and III slightly from the original quilt to make them proportional to the overall design.

Borders: For first border, cut four 1⅛"-wide strips from print fabric, two 47¼" long and two 64¼" long. Sew shorter strips to top and bottom of quilt top, then longer strips to sides, making ¼" seams.

For second (pieced) border, make templates for ⅞" and 1¼" triangles and 1¼" square, following directions above. Cut 532 ⅞" triangles from white fabric, 258 1¼" triangles from green fabric, and four squares from red fabric, adding seam allowance. Make rectangular patches by sewing two white triangles to each green triangle, matching a long white edge to each short green edge. Make square patches by sewing four white triangles to each red square as shown. Join rectangular patches into strips, making two strips of 55 patches each and two strips of 73 patches each. Join square patches to ends of longer strips. Sew shorter strips to top and

bottom of quilt top, then longer strips to sides, easing to fit if necessary and making ¼" seams.

For third border, cut four 1⅛"-wide strips from green fabric, two 52" long and two 69" long. Sew shorter strips to top and bottom, longer strips to sides as before. For fourth border, cut four 1⅜"-wide strips from red fabric, two 53¼" long and two 70¾" long. Sew on as before. Quilt top should measure 55" × 70¾".

Lining: From lining fabric, cut two pieces 28" × 70¾". Sew together on long edges with ½" seam to make lining 55" × 70¾". Cut batting same size.

Quilting: Using yardstick and tailor's chalk, mark grid pattern over main part of quilt top, using A and B squares as guides; lines will be 1" apart. Place lining flat, wrong side up. Place batting on top and anchor to lining by crossing two long stitches in center. Place quilt top on batting, right side up, and pin. Baste generously through all thicknesses, lengthwise, crosswise, and diagonally. Using white thread in needle, hand-quilt on marked lines. (See Quilting Stitch Detail on page 101.) Start in center and quilt one line out to both edges. Returning to center, quilt opposite line out to edges. Continue in this manner, working from center out. Quilt around each border.

FINISHING: From red fabric, cut four strips 1½" wide, two 55" long and two 71¼" long. On each, press under one long edge ¼". Pin shorter strips to top and bottom of quilt, right sides facing and matching raw edges; stitch in place with ¼" seam. Turn strips to wrong side and slip-stitch pressed edge to lining. Sew longer strips to sides in same manner, turning in ends ¼".

Country Christmas Hanging

Calico trees in shades of blue, polka-dot smoke and little, brightly embroidered figures—worked in easy stitches—make this quilted wall hanging particularly charming. Designed with Christmas in mind, it can represent the holiday spirit all year long, or save it for a special appearance at holiday time.

SIZE: 37½″ × 47″.

EQUIPMENT: Colored pencil. Pencil. Ruler. Scissors. Dressmaker's tracing (carbon) paper. Dry ball-point pen or tracing wheel. Sewing and embroidery needles. Iron. Quilting frame (optional). Tape.

MATERIALS: For background: Cotton fabric, 36″ wide, ½ yard light blue, 1 yard white. For appliqués: calico, 44″ wide, in four shades of blue (pale, light, bright*, dark), ¼ yard each; pale blue and a white in textured weaves, light blue with white dots, ⅛ yard each. For border: bright blue calico,* 44″ wide, ⅝ yard. For lining: soft fabric, 44″ wide, 1⅓ yards. White and matching sewing thread. Six-strand embroidery floss, 1 skein each: light and bright blue, black, gray, white, yellow, gold, peach, red, light, medium and dark brown, beige, olive and bright green. Batting.

*Note: We used the same bright blue calico for borders as we did for appliqués.

DIRECTIONS: Pattern for hanging is in two parts. Using sharp colored pencil, draw lines across each half of pattern, connecting grid lines. Enlarge pattern pieces, including heavy lines, light lines, and dotted lines, on paper ruled in 2″ squares (see Patterns, page 97); tape together. Heavy lines indicate appliqués; light lines, embroidery; dotted lines, quilting.

Background: Using pattern, cut sky from light blue fabric and ground from white, adding ½″ seam allowance along inner edge (horizon) of each piece. Turn under seam allowance of white ground piece, clipping as necessary, and press flat. Place pieces together, with ground overlapping sky for ½″. Pin, baste, slip-stitch in place, making background 36″ × 45½″.

Appliqués: Using dressmaker's carbon and dry ball-point pen, transfer appliqué pattern to background. Following directions for Appliqué on page 100, cut and prepare appliqué pieces; cut trees and bushes from the four shades of blue calico (see pattern and color photograph), houses and rooftops from textured pale blue and white, smoke from dotted blue, and clouds from remnants of white background fabric. Pin, baste, and slip-stitch appliqués in place.

Embroidery: Replace pattern on background and transfer embroidery designs. Using all six strands of floss in needle, embroider as follows (see Stitch Details on page 103 and color photograph for colors). Work large solid areas (garments, fence rail, horses) with split stitch; use a single row of split stitch for skates and to outline fence. Work smaller areas (faces, fur trim) with satin stitch. Work single lines (cross on steeple, window frames) with straight stitch. Use French knots for dots. Couch horse's rein with sewing thread.

Quilting: Transfer quilting lines (dotted lines) of pattern to landscape. Cut lining fabric 37½″ × 47″; cut single layer of batting same size. Lay lining out flat, wrong side up; place batting on top; center landscape on batting, right side up. Pin pieces together with large safety pins. Baste generously lengthwise, crosswise, diagonally in both directions and around perimeter. Start quilting in center and work around and outward, using matching thread in each area. (See Quilting Stitch Detail on page 101.) Making stitches ¼″ apart, quilt on marked lines for cloud details, hill contours and skating pond; fill roads and path with parallel lines ¼″ apart. Making stitches and rows ½″ apart, quilt in rows over remainder of hanging, skipping over clouds, rooftops, and figures; follow hill contours as much as possible and keep sky lines slightly wavy. Quilt around each figure and take a few stitches within the figure, concealed in the embroidery. Stitch all around top, ½″ from edge of fabric.

FINISHING: From bright blue calico, cut four border strips 4″ wide, two 47″ long (piecing for length) and two 38½″ long. Turn under all long edges ½″ and press; turn under ends of short strips ½″ and press. Fold each strip in half lengthwise, right side out, and press lightly. Enclose sides of hanging in long strips, overlapping edges of landscape and slip-stitch edges to front and back. Add short strips to top and bottom in same manner; slip-stitch ends closed.

Gingham Dog
and Calico Cat Quilt

Two lovable nursery pals are multiplied by three for six bedtime friends in bright calico or gingham. Add winsome faces with simple embroidery and frame in cheerful yellow calico, and this will please cat and dog lovers of all ages.

SIZES: 33¾" × 44¼".

EQUIPMENT: Scissors. Ruler. Pencils. Thin, stiff cardboard. Tailor's chalk. Paper for patterns. Dressmaker's (carbon) tracing paper. Tracing wheel or dry ball-point pen. Sewing and quilting needles. Quilting frame (optional).

MATERIALS: (All fabrics should be washable cotton or cotton blends.) Yellow and red calico, 36" wide, 8¾ yards (includes lining). Small amounts (about 6" × 9") of three ginghams and three calicos; scraps of fabric in red and contrasting solid colors. Red gingham for binding, ¼ yard. White fabric, 36" wide, ⅝ yard. White and matching sewing threads. One skein black cotton embroidery floss. Polyester or cotton batting.

DIRECTIONS: Read General Directions on pages 97–102. Quilt is constructed of six appliquéd blocks set with calico background.

Appliqués: Enlarge dog and cat patterns on paper ruled in 1" squares. (See Patterns, page 97.) Make a separate cardboard pattern for each appliqué piece (heavy lines on patterns): for dog—body, hind legs, head, two ears, tongue, five parts of bow; for cat—body, hind legs, tail, head, five parts of bow. Following directions in Appliqué on page 100, cut and prepare appliqué pieces, using a different gingham for each of three dogs and a different calico for each of three cats; cut bow pieces

in a contrasting solid color for each. Cut three dog's tongues from red.

Blocks: From white fabric, cut six pieces 9³⁄₁₆" × 9½", adding ¼" seam allowance all around. Using dressmaker's carbon and tracing wheel (or dry ball-point pen), transfer main outlines of dog to center of three white blocks and cat to remaining three blocks, placing 9³⁄₁₆" edges of blocks at sides.

Pin, baste, and slip-stitch appliqués in place, starting with pieces that will be overlapped by others.

Embroidery: See Stitch Details on page 103. Transfer embroidery pattern (light lines on pattern and noses, eyes and pupils) to appliquéd dogs and cats. Using full six strands of black embroidery floss, embroider eyelashes in straight stitch and remaining lines in outline stitch; embroider eye pupils and noses in satin stitch.

Background and Assembling: From yellow calico, cut four strips 2" × 9½" and one strip 2" × 31½", adding ¼" seam allowance all around. Sew appliquéd blocks into two vertical rows of three blocks each, with a short joining strip between blocks; make one row dog, cat, dog, and other row cat, dog, cat. Join rows, with long strip between. Piece should measure 21" × 31½", plus outside seam allowance.

For borders, cut two pieces from yellow calico 6" × 21" and two pieces 6" × 43½",

adding ¼″ seam allowance all around. Sew shorter pieces to top and bottom of quilt top, then longer pieces to sides. Quilt top should measure 33½″ × 44″, including outside seam allowance.

Lining: Cut lining 33½″ × 44″. Cut batting same size.

Quilting: With ruler and tailor's chalk, mark quilting lines as follows: On white background, mark diagonal lines 1⅜″ apart, alternating direction of lines from block to block as shown in illustration. Mark a square around each block, ¼″ away from seams. In each row of blocks, mark lines to connect squares drawn. Mark two X's in center of long joining strip, connecting corners of blocks as shown.

For border quilting design, cut a piece of cardboard 3¾″ square. Starting at upper left area of border, place square as a diamond with two opposite corners of pattern centered on seam joining top and side borders; draw around with tailor's chalk. Continuing to the right, draw around diamond four more times with adjacent points touching; corners of fifth diamond will be on seam joining top and right borders. Repeat pattern on bottom border. Fill in side borders with same pattern, making seven diamonds on each side border; start by placing one side of pattern against side of first diamond drawn. Extend lines to corners of quilt top to complete pattern.

Make another cardboard pattern 1¾″ square. Place pattern in center of all squares drawn and mark around with tailor's chalk. Cut pattern in half diagonally for a triangle pattern. Place triangle inside larger triangles (with 1″ margins) all around both outer and inner edges of border, and mark around.

Following general quilting directions on pages 100–101, pin and baste quilt top, batting, and lining together. Quilt around each separate appliqué piece and around embroidery defining front legs, noses, eyes, cats' mouths, and dogs' tongues; quilt on all marked lines.

FINISHING: From red gingham, cut bias strips 1¼″ wide; sew together to make strip about 158″ long for binding. With right sides together, and with ¼″ seams, sew strips to front of quilt. Turn strip to back of quilt, turn in raw edge ¼″, and slip-stitch to lining, making ⅜″-wide binding on front and back. Press edges.

Sunbonnet Sue Quilt Set

Everyone's sweetheart and her pet kitten are framed by fourteen pink-and-blue Windblown Star pieced blocks. The edge is scalloped in Dresden Plate patchwork, and appliquéd flowers surround the center design. Complete this portrait of innocence with matching pillow shams.

In this close-up, note how quilted flowers and leaves echo the appliqués.

SIZE: Quilt, about 92¾″ × 87″. Pillow shams, about 22″ × 26″ each.

EQUIPMENT: Pencil. Ruler. Brown paper, tracing paper, and graph paper, for patterns. Thin, stiff cardboard. Glue. Scissors. Dressmaker's tracing (carbon) paper. Tracing wheel or dry ball-point pen. Straight pins.

Sewing and quilting needles. Sewing machine with zigzag attachment. Iron.

MATERIALS: Closely woven cotton fabrics, 44″ wide: white, 5½ yards; white-on-pink dotted, 2½ yards; white-on-blue dotted, 2 yards; pink-on-white print and blue-on-white print, 2 yards each. Scraps of the following fabrics: light blue, medium blue, light green, medium green, flesh color, additional pink-on-white and blue-on-white prints, pink calico. Fabric for lining, 44″ wide, 5¼ yards for quilt, ¾ yard for two shams. Light green bias tape, ½″ wide, 6¼ yards. Pink double-fold bias tape, ¼″ wide, 16½ yards. White pre-ruffled cotton eyelet trim, 2″ wide, 4¾ yards. Sewing thread to match fabrics and trims. Blue quilting thread. White flat elastic ¼″ wide, 3 yards. Batting.

Sunbonnet Sue Quilt

DIRECTIONS: Quilt is made up of appliquéd center block framed with 14 pieced blocks, plus plain, pieced, and appliquéd borders.

Appliquéd Block: Draw lines across appliqué pattern, connecting grid lines. Enlarge pattern by copying on paper ruled in 2″ squares. (See Patterns, page 97.) Heavy lines indicate individual appliqués, fine lines, machine embroidery; dotted lines are quilting patterns. Make separate tracings of quilted scroll and flower; set tracings aside. From white fabric, cut 23½″ × 34″ piece for background. Referring to color detail, transfer main outlines of appliqué designs to background, using dressmaker's carbon and tracing wheel. Referring to Appliqué (page 100), transfer individual appliqué pieces to fabrics, following color detail. Cut out pieces. Following directions for machine appliqué, pin, baste, and stitch pieces in place on background, using matching threads. After all pieces have been appliquéd, transfer fine embroidery lines and machine-embroider; fill in kitten's nose solidly.

Pieced Blocks: Mark pattern A on graph paper, following small diagram. Following Diagram 1, mark additional patterns on graph paper. B: 3″ square. C: half of B. D: half of C. Glue paper patterns to cardboard; let dry; cut carefully along marked lines for four templates. To mark patches, place template on wrong side of fabric with right angles or parallel edges on straight of goods. Draw around template with sharp pencil held at an outward angle. Mark as many patches as needed of one color at one time, leaving ½″

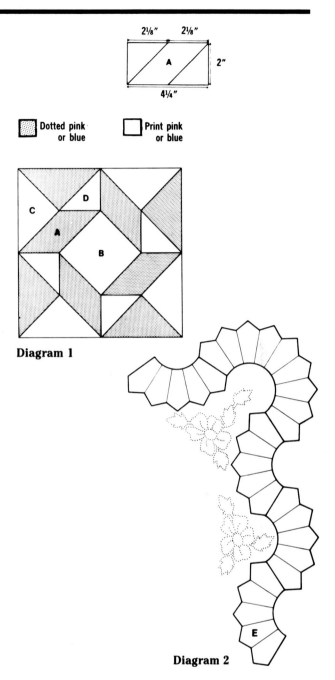

Dotted pink or blue   Print pink or blue

Diagram 1

Diagram 2

between two patches; mark along length of yard goods, close to one selvage, rather than across width, leaving the opposite side intact for cutting strips and borders later. On dotted pink and dotted blue fabrics, mark 28 each of A and C. On pink-on-white and blue-on-white prints, mark seven of B and 28 each of C and D. When all pieces are marked, cut out ¼″ outside pencil lines, for seam allowance; pencil line will be stitching line. To join pieces for a block, place them together with right sides facing, matching one edge. Stitch on marked line; press seam to one side under darker color. Referring to Diagram 1, join adjacent C's. Join A's and D's in pairs. Attach C's and B to A-D strips. Block should measure 9″ square, including outside seam allowance. Make seven pink blocks and seven blue blocks in this manner.

Assembling: When all blocks are completed, arrange them as shown in color photograph. To join blocks, cut 14 strips 2½″ × 9″ from white fabric. Place strips between adjacent pieced blocks. Making ¼″ seams, join two blocks and three strips in turn to complete top and bottom of pieced "frame." Join five blocks and four strips to complete each side. Join top and bottom, then sides of frame to appliquéd block, completing main part of quilt top. Piece should measure 40½″ × 51″, including seam allowance. (Measure your own piece and adjust length of following border strips if necessary.)

Plain Borders: Cut and join four sets of border strips in turn as follows, piecing together as necessary; dimensions include seam allowance. For first three sets, sew longer strips to sides of quilt top with ¼″ seams; sew shorter strips to top and bottom. First border: From white fabric, cut two strips 2½″ × 51″, two strips 2½″ × 44½″. Second border: From dotted pink fabric, cut two strips 3¼″ × 55″, two strips 3¼″ × 50″. Third border: From dotted blue fabric, cut two strips 3¼″ × 60½″, two strips 3¼″ × ·55½″. Outer border: From white fabric, cut one strip 3¼″ × 55½″, two strips 15¼″ × 68¾″, and one strip 15¼″ × 85″. Sew 3¼″-wide strip to top of quilt. Sew two short strips to sides. Sew long strip to bottom. Piece should measure 85″ × 83½″.

Pieced Border: Following directions for pieced blocks, trace pattern E and make template. Use template to cut 223 patches from pink and blue yard goods and scraps, adding seam allowance. Alternating prints at random, join pieces on their long edges to make fan shapes as shown in Diagram 2; make 41 groups of five pieces each and two groups of nine pieces each. For bottom, join 13 five-piece groups, alternating direction as shown in diagram. For each side, join 14 groups in

same manner. Join sides and bottom to nine-piece corners, making three-sided border. Place border on quilt top, overlapping outer edge of white border with inner edge of pieced border; see illustration. Following

APPLIQUÉD BLOCK

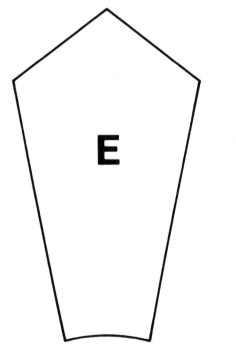

E

directions for hand appliqué, pin, baste, and stitch inner edge in place. Trim side and bottom edges of white border to match pieced border if necessary; trim pieced border at top.

Appliquéd Border: Referring to color photograph, pin green bias tape to sides and bottom of white border for wavy vine; piece together as necessary; trim ends even with top edge. Stitch tape close to long edges, using machine set for short straight stitches. Using appliqué patterns, cut out pieces for 49 machine-appliqué flowers from assorted pink and blue yard goods and scraps; cut 115 leaves from green fabrics. Arrange flowers and leaves above, below, and over vine as shown, leaving space for quilted flowers between appliqués and pieced border. Use pencil to mark leaf and flower stems. Pin, baste, and stitch appliqués in place. After all pieces have been appliquéd, machine-embroider over fine lines and pencil lines.

Quilting: Replace enlarged pattern over appliquéd block and transfer quilting patterns. Continue to mark scroll around appliquéd block, on joining strips and white inner border. Mark a flower in each corner of appliquéd block. Rule across pink and blue borders, marking off 2¾" squares. Referring to Diagram 2, transfer flower to bottom and sides of white outer border; mark one flower in each bottom corner, adding additional leaf as shown.

Cut lining fabric in half crosswise for two pieces 94½" long. Join together at one long edge with ½" seam to make piece 87" × 94½". Cut batting same size. Place lining flat, wrong side up. Place batting on top. Anchor batting to lining by crossing two long stitches in center. Center quilt top over batting. Pin and baste through all layers, lengthwise, crosswise, and diagonally in both directions.

Starting in center and working outward in all directions, quilt on quilting lines and around all appliqués, patch pieces, and borders; stitch close to seams. Use blue quilting thread. (See Quilting Stitch Detail, page 101.) Trim lining and batting to match quilt top.

FINISHING: Starting at upper left corner of quilt and working down, around, and up to upper right corner, pin pink bias tape to quilt top, enclosing edges; place wider side of tape on lining side. Topstitch in place. Bind top edge of quilt in same manner, folding ends under ¼" before stitching.

Pillow Shams

DIRECTIONS: For sham top, make two pink and two blue pieced blocks, following directions for quilt top. Arrange blocks as shown in illustration. To join blocks, cut from white fabric two strips 2½" × 9" and three strips 2½" × 19½". Join a pink and a blue block to a 9" strip for top row; repeat for bottom row. Join rows with a 19½" strip. Sew remaining strips to opposite sham edges for side borders.

Quilting: Mark scroll on joining strips and borders. From lining fabric, cut 19½" × 23½" piece. Cut batting same size. Assemble pieces and quilt, following directions for quilt top.

To Make Sham: Cut eyelet trim in half for two 2⅜-yard lengths. Pin one length of eyelet around sham top, right sides facing and straight edges even; overlap ends. Stitch, making ¼" seam. From dotted pink fabric, cut 3¾" × 90" strip for ruffle. Stitch ends together, right sides facing and with ¼" seam, forming a ring; turn to right side. Press one long edge ¼" to wrong side twice; topstitch. Baste close to raw edge of ruffle; pull basting gently, gathering it to fit sham edges. With right side of ruffle facing wrong side of eyelet, pin gathers to straight edges of eyelet; stitch. From white fabric, cut 7" × 86½" strip. Stitch ends together to form a ring as for ruffle. Press one long edge ¼" then ½" to wrong side; topstitch. Cut elastic in half for two 1½-yard lengths. Pin elastic over stitching on wrong side of ring, stretching it to fit; overlap ends. Stitch, using machine set for wide zigzag stitches; reset machine for straight stitches. Pin and stitch raw edge to sham top as for ruffle; turn to right side.

Embroidered Tree
and House Pillows

Country scenes in patchwork—fresh calico colors enriched with patches and borders of blue-green velveteen. Bits of embroidery add flowers and fruit. What easier way is there to bring a bit of the country to a city room?

House Pillow

SIZE: 18½″ × 19″.

EQUIPMENT: Light and dark-colored pencils. Ruler. Scissors. Thin, stiff cardboard. Sewing and embroidery needles. Glue.

MATERIALS: Dark blue-green velveteen, 45″ wide, ⅝ yard. Small amounts of three floral prints with backgrounds of tan (A), white (B), and blue (C). Scraps of solid red (D), turquoise (E), and blue (F). Matching sewing thread. Six-strand embroidery floss, less than a skein of green, light blue, red, and pink. Muslin. Batting. Fiberfill for stuffing.

DIRECTIONS: Read General Directions on pages 97–102.

Patterns: Enlarge pattern by copying on paper ruled in 1″ squares, to make block 11″ × 11½″ (see Patterns, page 97). Glue pattern to cardboard. Cut on marked lines for individual patch patterns.

Patch Pieces: Marking patterns on wrong side of fabric and adding ¼″ seam allowance all around, cut 19 patch pieces; for fabric colors, match letters of colors given in Materials to letters on pattern.

Right sides facing, join patch pieces to assemble house block. Piece should measure 11½″ × 12″, including outside seam allowance.

Quilting: Cut batting and muslin for backing, each 11½″ × 12″. Following general quilting directions on pages 100–101, pin and baste backing, batting, and house block together. With two strands of floss in needle, quilt along both sides of all seams; quilt crosslines on window, as shown on pattern. Use green floss for chimneys, door, and window; red for house; pink for sky; light blue for roof.

Embroidery: Referring to pattern and Stitch Details on page 103, embroider as follows, with two strands of floss in needle and going through all layers. On front of house, flanking door, make red satin-stitch flowers with green chain-stitch stems and leaves. On door, make pink satin-stitch flowers with blue chain-stitch stems and blue satin-stitch leaves. Make doorknob in green satin stitch. Where house and ground join, make zigzag line in green featherstitch.

Borders: From blue-green velveteen, cut two pieces 4½″ × 11½″ and two pieces 4½″ × 20″. Sew shorter strips to sides of house block, with ¼″ seams, then longer strips to top and bottom. With light blue floss, make medium-length stitches ⅛″ from seams, as shown. Pillow front should measure 19½″ × 20″.

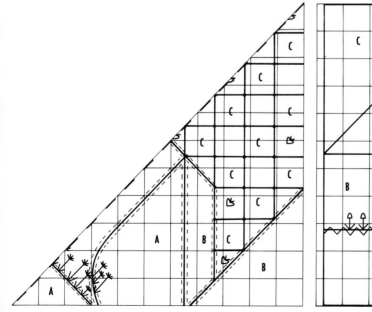

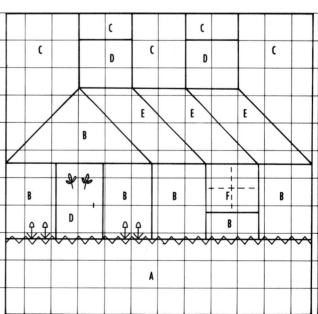

Pillow: From velveteen, cut piece for pillow back, 19½″ × 20″. Right sides together and with ½″ seams, sew pillow front and back together; leave 6″ opening in center of one side. Turn to right side, pushing out corners. Stuff pillow fully. Slip-stitch opening closed.

Embroidered Tree Pillow

SIZE: 15½″ square.

EQUIPMENT: See House Pillow.

MATERIALS: Dark blue-green velveteen, 45″ wide, ½ yard. Small amounts of three floral prints with backgrounds of white (A), blue (B), and red (C). Matching sewing thread. Six-strand embroidery floss, less than a skein of dark green, chartreuse, red, light blue, pink, and yellow. Muslin. Batting. Fiberfill.

DIRECTIONS: Read General Directions on pages 97–102.

Patterns: Enlarge pattern on paper ruled in 1″ squares (See Patterns, page 97); complete half-pattern indicated by dash lines to make block 11″ square. Glue pattern to cardboard. Cut on marked lines for individual patch patterns.

Patch Pieces: See House Pillow. Cut 53 patch pieces, cutting nonlettered pieces from blue-green velveteen. Tree block should measure 11½″ square, including outside seam allowance.

Quilting: Cut batting and muslin for backing, each 11½″ square. Following general quilting directions on pages 100–101, pin and baste backing, batting, and tree block together. With two strands of floss in needle, quilt only where indicated by short dash lines on pattern; use dark green floss along blue-green edges of tree and light blue floss along blue and white edges. Following directions on page 102, make tufts in foliage where indicated by dots on pattern, using full six strands of dark green floss in needle; clip yarn to leave ¼″ ends.

Embroidery: Referring to pattern and Stitch Details on page 103, embroider as follows, with two strands of floss in needle and going through all layers. In foliage, make red satin-stitch fruit, with chartreuse lazy-daisy leaves. On ground, make red, blue, pink, and yellow flowers in radiating straight stitch. Make leaves and stems in chartreuse chain stitch.

Borders, Pillow: See House Pillow. Cut border pieces 3″ × 11½″ and 3″ × 16½″. Stitch with red floss. Pillow front should measure 16½″ square. Cut backing same size.

PART II
AFGHANS

Afghans to crochet. Afghans to knit. And patterns varied enough to suit every taste and be attractive in any setting. For crocheters, there are picture afghans—playful kittens or nautical motifs—and a lovely all-white afghan delicately decorated with a field of roses. For knitters, there is a sporty argyle pattern from Scotland and the lovely Irish Inishmore.

Autumn Windows Afghan

Three brilliant panels in golds and oranges borrowed from autumn leaves are set like stained-glass windows in frames of brown. Long single crochets in six graduating lengths form a pattern reminiscent of bargello work in needlepoint.

SIZE: 64" × 78".

MATERIALS: Yarns of worsted weight, 2 4-ounce balls each medium brown (A), burnt orange (B), tangerine (C), dark gold (D), yellow (E); 3 balls off-white (F), 7 balls dark brown (G). Crochet hook size H (5mm).

GAUGE: 3 sts = 1". (To test gauge, see page 108.)

AFGHAN: COLOR PANEL (make 3): With A, ch 36.

Row 1: Sc in 2nd ch from hook and in each ch across—35 sc. Ch 1, turn.

Rows 2–8: Sc in each sc across. Ch 1, turn each row. Cut A.

Row 9: With B, sc in first sc, * sc in next st 1 row below, sc in next st 2 rows below, sc in next st 3 rows below, sc in next st 4 rows below, sc in next st 5 rows below, sc in next st 6 rows below, sc in next st, repeat from * across, end sc in last st 6 rows below. Ch 1, turn.

Rows 10–16: Sc in each st across. Ch 1, turn each row. Cut B.

Row 17: With C, sc in first st 6 rows below, * sc in next st 5 rows below, sc in next st 4 rows below, sc in next st 3 rows below, sc in next st 2 rows below, sc in next st 1 row below, sc in next st, sc in next st 6 rows below, repeat from * across, end sc in last sc. Ch 1, turn.

Rows 18–24: Sc in each st across. Ch 1, turn each row. Cut C.

Rows 25–32: With D, repeat rows 9–16.

Rows 33–40: With E, repeat rows 17–24.

Rows 41–48: With F, repeat rows 9–16.

Rows 49–56: With A, repeat rows 17–24. Continue to work panel by repeating rows 9–24 and repeating colors as established until there are 6 complete patterns of colors A to F. With A, work row 17 across. End off.

BORDERS: With G, ch 186.

Row 1: Hdc in 2nd ch from hook and in each ch across—185 hdc. Ch 1, turn each row.

Row 2: Hdc in each hdc across.

Rows 3–16: Repeat row 3.

Row 17: Hdc in 20 sts, ch 1, turn. Work even on 20 sts until piece is same length as color panel, end at inside edge. Cut yarn.
  *Sk next 35 sts on row 15; with G, hdc in next 20 sts. Work even in hdc until piece is same number of rows as first border piece. Repeat from * twice more. Do not end off last border piece. Ch 1, turn.

Top Border: Hdc in each hdc of border, * ch 35, hdc in each hdc of next border piece, repeat from * across. Ch 1, turn. Work even in hdc on 185 sts for 16 rows. End off.

FINISHING: Sew borders to color panels. With G, work 3 rnds of sc around afghan, working 3 sc in each corner each rnd and working back lp of each sc on rnds 2 and 3.

Folk Art Afghan

Classic early American motifs—stylized flowers, animals, birds, a charming couple—give this coverlet its delightful traditional mood. Designs are cross-stitched on squares of afghan-stitch crochet.

SIZE: 48″ × 66″.

MATERIALS: Knitting worsted weight yarn, 13 4-ounce balls white. For embroidery, sport yarn, 1 2-ounce ball each of red, light blue and medium blue. Afghan hook size 4 mm (F). Tapestry needles.

GAUGE: 9 sts = 2″, 4 rows = 1″. (To test gauge, see page 108.)

AFGHAN STITCH SQUARE: (make 12): Ch 67.

Row 1: Keeping all lps on hook, sk first ch from hook, pull up a lp in 2nd ch from hook and in each ch across —67 lps.

To Work Lps Off: Yo hook, pull through first lp * yo hook, pull through next 2 lps, repeat from * across until 1 lp remains. Lp that remains on hook always counts as first st of next row.

Row 2: Keeping all lps on hook, sk first vertical bar (lp on hook is first st), pull up a lp under next vertical bar and under each vertical bar across. Work lps off as before. Repeat row 2 until there are 60 rows. Sl st in each vertical bar across. End off. Block square.

EMBROIDERY: Embroider squares in cross-stitch before assembling them. (See page 103.) Following chart 1 for border, work border around each square. Beg at lower right-hand corner of chart and square, work first medium blue st on 2nd row of square and 2nd st. Following chart 2, make 4 squares for corners of afghan, beginning at each A on chart 1 for each corner square.

    Following chart 3, make 2 squares for center top and center bottom of afghan, beginning first row of sts at B on chart 1.

    Following chart 4, make 2 squares for center of afghan, 2nd and 3rd rows, beginning first row of sts from C to C on chart 1.

    Following chart 5, make 2 squares for right edge, 2nd row, and left edge, 3rd row, beginning first row of skirt sts from D to D on chart 1. Mouths on charts 5 and 6 are small straight red sts.

    Following chart 6, make 2 squares for right edge, 3rd row, and left edge, 2nd row, working first row of feet at E on chart 1.

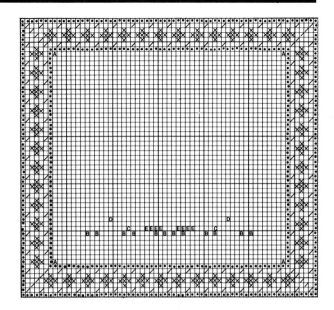

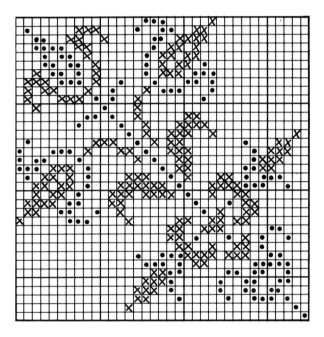

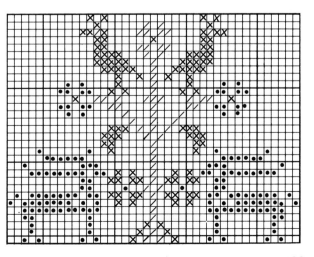

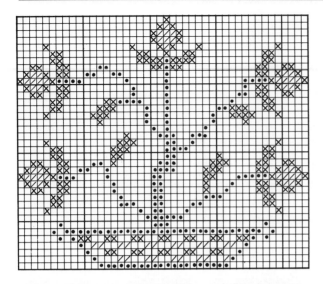

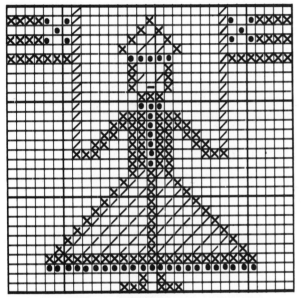

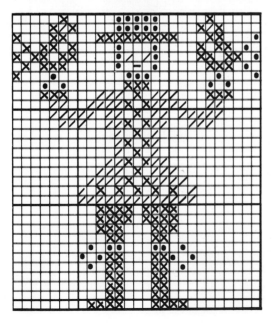

JOINING SQUARES: See diagram for joining squares.

First Row: Join yarn in upper left corner of square 1, * ch 6, sk 3 rows on left side of square, sc in next row, repeat from * to lower left corner of square, ch 4, sc in lower right corner of square 2; ** ch 3, sc in next ch-6 lp, ch 3, sk 3 rows on right side edge of square 2, repeat from ** to top, ch 4, sl st in joining st at top of square 1; end off.

Join yarn in upper left corner of square 2, work lps and join square 3 to square 2, as first 2 squares were joined. In same way, join next 3 rows of squares.

JOINING ROWS: Join yarn in upper right corner of square 1. * Ch 6, sk 3 sts on top edge of square, sc in next st, repeat from * across top of square, end 2 sts from corner, ch 6, sc in ch-4 lp between squares, repeat from first * across, end sc in left corner of square 3, ch 4, sc in lower left corner of square 6. ** Ch 3, sc in next ch-6 lp, ch 3, sk 3 sts on lower edge of square, sc in next st, repeat from ** across to lower right corner of square 4, ch 4, sl st in upper right corner of square 1. End off.

Join 3rd and 2nd rows of squares tog in same way.

Join 4th and 3rd rows of squares tog in same way.

FINISHING: From right side, work 1 row of sc around outer edge of afghan, working 1 sc in each st or row, 4 sc in each ch-4 lp, and 3 sc in each corner. Working from left to right, work reverse sc in each sc around.

12	11	10
9	8	7
6	5	4
3	2	1

Cool Reflections Afghan

The subtle shading of color from dark to light, light to dark characterizes the ripple afghan—beautiful and easy to make.

SIZE: 45" × 60".

MATERIALS: Sport yarn, 24 2-ounce skeins white. Aluminum crochet hook size E. Tapestry needle.

GAUGE: One square = 7½". (To test gauge, see page 108.)

SQUARE: (make 63): Ch 6, join with a sl st in first ch to form ring.

Rnd 1: Ch 3 (counts as first dc), 11 dc in ring, join with sl st to top of ch 3.

Rnd 2: Ch 2, hdc in same place as sl st, 2 hdc in each dc around—24 hdc, counting ch 2 as 1 hdc. Join.

Rnd 3: Ch 1, sc in same place as sl st, * ch 5, sk next 2 hdc, sc in next hdc, repeat from * 6 times, end ch 5, join in first sc—8 lps.

Rnd 4: *In next lp make (sc, hdc, 5 dc, hdc, sc), repeat from * 7 times—8 petals. Join in first sc.

Rnd 5: *Ch 5; holding next petal forward and working behind it, sc around bar of next sc of rnd 3, inserting hook from back to front to back, repeat from * 6 times, ch 5, do not join.

Rnd 6: * In next lp work (sc, hdc, 7 dc, hdc, sc) repeat from * 7 times—8 petals. Sl st in first sc.

Rnd 7: * Ch 7; holding next petal forward and working behind it, sc around bar of next sc of rnd 5, repeat from * 6 times, ch 7, do not join.

Rnd 8: * In next lp work (sc, hdc, 9 dc, hdc, sc), repeat from * 7 times. Sl st in first sc.

Rnd 9: Ch 7, * (dc, ch 4, dc) in 5th dc of next petal for corner, ch 4, dc between petals, ch 4, sc in 5th dc of next petal, ch 4, dc between petals, ch 4, repeat from * 3 times, end last repeat ch 4, sl st in 3rd ch of ch 7.

Rnd 10: Sl st in next ch-4 sp, ch 3, 3 dc in same sp, ch 1; * (2 dc, ch 3, 2 dc) in corner sp, ch 1, 4 dc in next sp, (ch 1, 3 dc in next sp) twice, ch 1, 4 dc in next sp. ch 1, repeat from * 3 times, end last repeat, ch 1, sl st in top of ch 3.

Rnd 11: Sl st in each st across to next corner sp, (ch 3, dc, ch 3, 2 dc) in same sp, * ch 1, sk next 2 dc of corner, dc in each of next 4 dc, ch 1, (dc in each of next 3 dc, ch 1) twice, dc in each of next 4 dc, ch 1, (2 dc, ch 3, 2 dc) in corner sp, repeat from * twice, ch 1, sk next 2 dc of corner, dc in each of next 4 dc, ch 1, (dc in each of next 3 dc, ch 1) twice, dc in top of ch 3, dc over sl sts into each of next 3 dc, ch 1, sl st in top of ch 3.

Rnd 12: Sl st across to corner sp, (ch 3, 2 dc, ch 3, 3 dc) in same sp, * ch 1, sk 2 dc of corner, dc in each of next 4 dc, ch 1, (dc in each of next 3 dc, ch 1) twice, dc in each of next 4 dc, ch 1, (3 dc, ch 3, 3 dc) in corner sp, repeat from * 3 times, end last repeat dc in each of 4 dc, ch 1, sl st in top of ch 3.

Rnd 13: Sl st across to corner sp, (ch 3, 2 dc, ch 3, 3 dc) in same sp, * ch 2, sk 3 dc of corner, dc in each of next 4 dc, ch 1, (dc in each of next 3 dc, ch 1) twice, dc in each of next 4 dc, ch 2, (3 dc, ch 3, 3 dc) in corner sp, repeat from * 3 times, end last repeat dc in each of 4 dc, ch 2, sl st in top of ch 3. End off. Weave in all loose ends.

FINISHING: Thread tapestry needle with yarn. Hold 2 squares with right sides tog: join yarn in upper right-hand corner of one square, sew across, picking up center two strands only (front lps of sts). Carefully match each st and corners. Join rest of squares in same way to make 7 strips of 9 squares each; then join strips across long sides. Lightly steam joinings.

Edging:

Rnd 1: From right side, sc in any corner sp, ch 5, sc in same sp, * ch 5, sc in next sp, repeat from * around, being sure to count square corner on each side of every joining as a sp, and working sc, ch 5, sc in each corner of afghan. Sl st in first sc.

Rnd 2: Work petal of (sc, hdc, 5 dc, hdc, sc) in corner sp and in each ch-5 sp around. Sl st in first sc. End off.

Florentine Afghan

Reminiscent of Florentine needlepoint, this afghan is almost completely embroidered in cross-stitch on afghan crochet panels, and can be made in one piece or in three separate panels.

SIZE: About 54″ × 72″.

MATERIALS: Knitting worsted weight yarns 13 4-ounce balls of brown (MC). For embroidery, 1 ball each of baby yellow (A), medium gold (B), dark gold (C), pale olive (D), medium olive (E), baby blue (F), wedgewood blue (G), marine blue (H), light rose (I), dark rose (J), burgundy (K). Afghan hook size I (5:50 mm). Crochet hook size H (5:00 mm). Tapestry needles.

GAUGE: 4 sts = 1″; 3 rows = 1″. (To test gauge, see page 108.)

Note: Afghan can be made in one piece or in 3 separate panels.

ONE-PIECE AFGHAN: With MC, ch 223. Work in Afghan Stitch on 223 sts, following directions, page 107, until 221 rows have been completed. Work sl st in each vertical bar across. End off.

AFGHAN IN PANELS: With MC, ch 71. Work in Afghan Stitch on 71 sts, following

directions, page 107, until 221 rows have been completed. Work sl st in each vertical bar across. End off. Make one more panel the same.

For center panel, with MC, ch 81. Work in Afghan Stitch on 81 sts until 221 rows have been completed. Work sl st in each vertical bar across. End off.

FINISHING: If afghan is made in panels, sew panels tog with MC having wider panel in center. With MC, work 1 row sc along each long edge of afghan. Following chart, embroider afghan in cross-stitch (see page 103): work from A to B twice, then from A to C once. When top of chart is reached, repeat from bottom of chart twice, then repeat from bottom of chart until top of afghan is reached.

Steam. For fringe, cut strands of all colors 10″. Using 2 strands of MC and 1 strand each of 3 colors, knot fringe in every other st across top and bottom of afghan, alternating the 4 color groups. Trim ends.

□ = MC
◪ = A
◉ = B
⊠ = C
⊡ = D
◪ = E
▽ = F
⊞ = G
⊟ = H
◪ = I
▣ = J
◪ = K

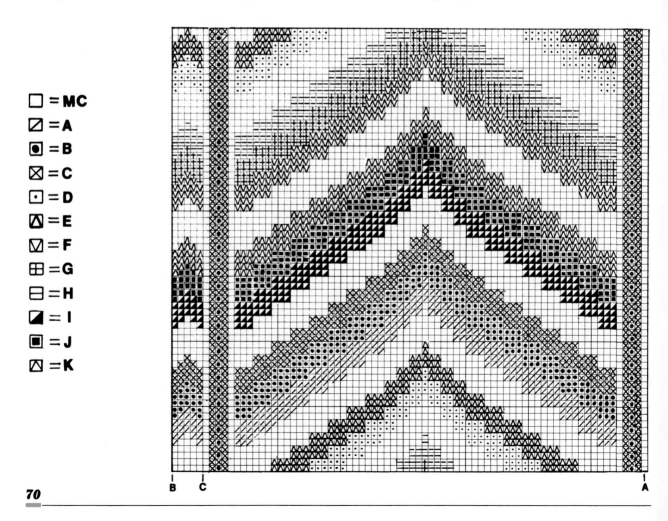

Heart Afghan

A hearts-and-flowers afghan in single crochet bears designs embroidered in cross-stitch. Dimensions are 51 inches by 66 inches, but it can be made in any convenient length or width. Make it for your valentine or for any collector of heart-patterned furnishings.

ONE-COLOR SQUARES

COLOR	NUMBER NEEDED
Blue	350
Green	7
Orange	10
Amber	50
Red	8
Yellow	6
White	41
Black	5
Steel Gray	4
Lt. Gold	41

TWO-COLOR SQUARES

COLORS	NUMBER NEEDED
Lt. Gold/Amber	1
Blue/Lt. Gold	4
Blue/White	14
Blue/Black	1
Blue/Red	6
Blue/Amber	14
Blue/Orange	8
Blue/Yellow	4
Blue/Green	5
Blue/Steel Gray	2
Amber/White	1
Orange/White	1
Orange/Amber	7
Orange/Green	1
Yellow/Green	1
Yellow/Red	1
Black/White	5
Steel Gray/White	2

COLOR KEY

	White
	Lt. Gold
	Blue
	Amber
1	Black
2	Green
3	Orange
4	Red

5	Yellow
6	Steel Gray
7	Lt. Gold/Amber
8	Blue/Lt. Gold
9	Blue/White
10	Blue/Black
11	Blue/Red
12	Blue/Orange
13	Blue/Yellow
14	Blue/Green

15	Blue/Steel Gray
16	Amber/White
17	Orange/Green
18	Orange/White
19	Orange/Amber
20	Yellow/Green
21	Yellow/Red
22	Black/White
23	Steel Gray/White
24	Amber/Blue

Heart Afghan

A hearts-and-flowers afghan in single crochet bears designs embroidered in cross-stitch. Dimensions are 51 inches by 66 inches, but it can be made in any convenient length or width. Make it for your valentine or for any collector of heart-patterned furnishings.

SIZE: 51″ × 66″.

MATERIALS: Knitting worsted, 11 100-gram (onc ounce equals 28.35 grams) balls white, 6 balls red. Crochet hook size H (5 mm). Large-eyed embroidery needle.

GAUGE: 4 sc = 1″; 4 rows = 1″. (To test gauge, see page 108.)

PANEL: (make 3): With white, ch 52.

Row 1: Sc in 2nd ch from hook and each ch across—51 sc. Ch 1, turn.

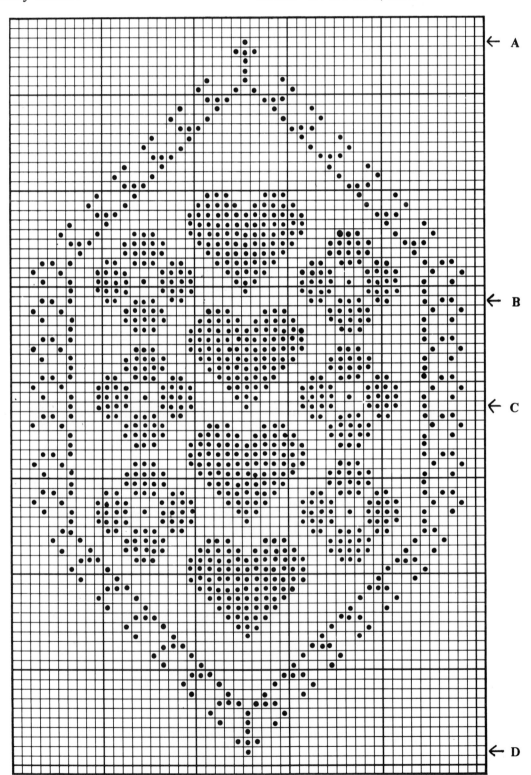

← A

← B

← C

← D

☐ White

⊡ Red

Row 2: Sc in each sc across. Ch 1, turn. Repeat row 2, 236 times more—238 rows. Omit ch 1; end off.

VERTICAL STRIP (make 4): With red, ch 12.

Row 1: Dc in 6th ch from hook, * ch 1, sk 1 ch, dc in next ch, repeat from * across. Ch 4, turn.

Row 2: Skip first dc (turning ch counts as first dc, ch 1), * (yo, pull up a lp) 4 times in next dc, yo, pull lp through all lps on hook, ch 1 (bobble made), ch 1, dc in next dc, ch 1, repeat from * once more, end with dc in top of turning ch. Ch 4, turn.

Row 3: * Dc in top of bobble, ch 1, dc in next dc, ch 1, repeat from * across, end with dc in turning ch. Ch 4, turn.

Repeat rows 2 and 3, 45 times more, then repeat row 2 once. Omit last ch 4.

FINISHING: Embroider panels in cross-stitch, following chart for design. Work from A to B, repeat from C to B 12 times then work from C to D to complete design.

Sew panels and vertical strips together alternately, with narrow strips at outer edges.

HORIZONTAL STRIP (make 2): With red, ch 192.

Row 1: (Yo, pull up a lp) 4 times in 6th ch from hook, yo, pull lp through all lps on hook, ch 1 (bobble made), * ch 1, sk 1 ch, dc in next ch, ch 1, sk 1 ch, bobble in next ch, repeat from * across, end ch 1, dc in last ch. Ch 4, turn.

Row 2: * Dc in top of bobble, ch 1, dc in next dc, ch 1, repeat from * across, end with dc in top of turning ch. Ch 4, turn.

Row 3: Sk first dc (turning ch counts as first dc, ch 1),* work bobble in next dc, ch 1, dc in next dc, ch 1, repeat from * across, end dc in turning ch. End off.

Sew horizontal strips to top and bottom of afghan.

Mallards In Fall Afghan

This ducky coverlet is executed in afghan-stitch crochet and embroidered with colorful cross-stitch mallards.

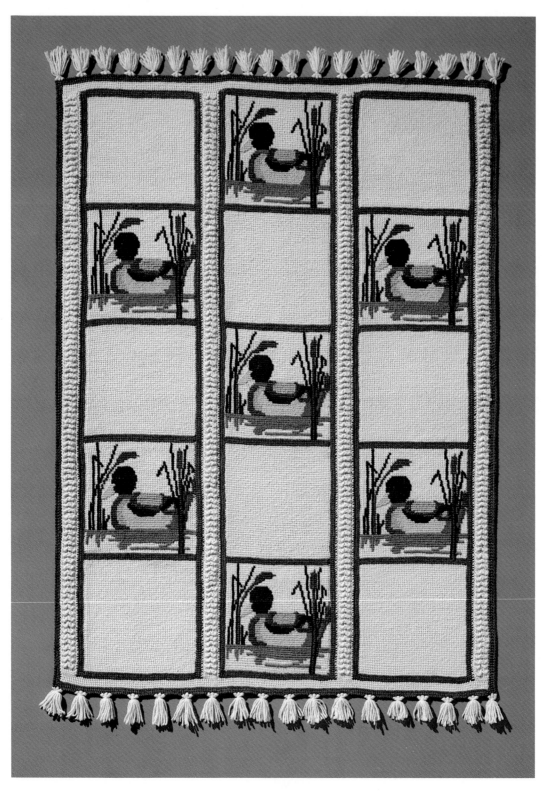

SIZE: 44″ × 62″, plus fringe.

MATERIALS: Knitting worsted, 17 3-ounce balls off-white, 5 balls warm brown, 1 ball medium blue. Yarns of worsted weight, 1 4-ounce ball each of honey, yellow, sea green, and tangerine. Two long afghan hooks size G (4¼ mm). Tapestry needle.

GAUGE: 6 sts = 1″; 14 rows = 3″. (To test gauge, see page 108.)

AFGHAN: PANEL (make 3): With afghan hook and warm brown, ch 62.

Row 1: Keeping all lps on hook, pull up a lp in 2nd ch from hook and in each ch across—62 lps on hook.

To Work Lps Off: Yo hook, pull through first lp, * yo hook, pull through next 2 lps, repeat from * across until 1 lp remains on hook. Lp that remains on hook counts as first st of next row.

Row 2: Keeping all lps on hook, sk first vertical bar, pull up a lp under next vertical bar and under each vertical bar across. Work lps off as before. Repeat row 2 for plain afghan stitch.

Row 3: Work in afghan stitch, change to off-white at end of row by pulling through last 2 lps on hook. Cut warm brown.

Rows 4–55: With off-white work in afghan stitch for 52 rows, change to warm brown at end of row 55.

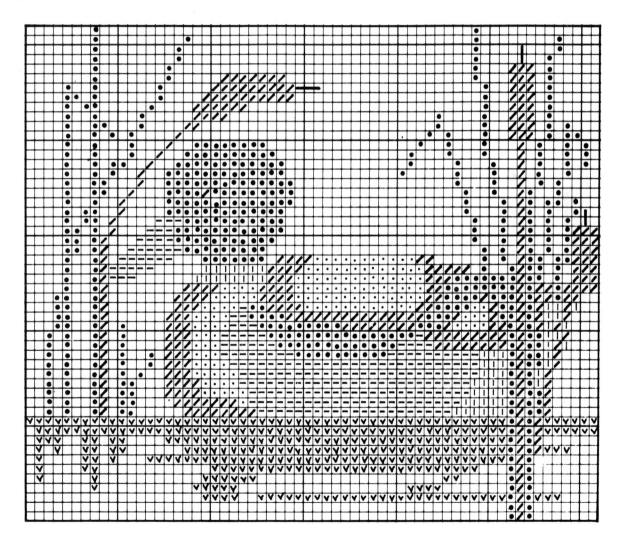

◿ Warm Brown	⊡ Honey	⊟ Sea Green	
ⱱ Medium Blue	⊟ Yellow	Ⅱ Tangerine	

Rows 56–58: With warm brown, work in afghan stitch for 3 rows, change to off-white at end of row 58.

Repeat rows 4–58, 4 times—5 blocks of off-white. When last 3 rows of warm brown have been completed, do not change to off-white. Sl st in each vertical bar of last row. End off.

Edging: With warm brown, pick up a lp in each row along side of panel. Work in afghan stitch for 3 rows. End off. Work edging along both sides of all 3 panels.

EMBROIDERY: Following chart, embroider off-white blocks in cross-stitch (see page 103). On center panel, embroider first, third and fifth blocks. On two side panels, embroider second and fourth blocks. Make straight stitches at top of cattails in brown.

BORDER PANEL (make 4): With off-white, ch 9.

Rows 1–3: Work in afghan stitch.

Row 4: Pull up a lp in next 3 vertical bars (4 lps on hook): yo hook 3 times, pull up a lp in 2nd bar of previous row, (yo and through 2 lps) 3 times (5 lps on hook); yo hook 3 times, pull up a lp in 8th bar of previous row, (yo and through 2 lps) 4 times (5 lps on hook), sk next vertical bar, pull up a lp in each of last 4 bars (9 lps on hook). Work lps off.

Row 5: Work in afghan stitch. Repeat rows 4 and 5 until border panel is same length as afghan panel. Sl st in each bar across. End off. With off-white, from wrong side, sc or sew border panels between afghan panels and on each side of afghan.

FINISHING: With off-white work 4 rows of afghan stitch across bottom edge of afghan. Change to warm brown, work 3 rows. End off. Work same border on top edge of afghan.

With warm brown, work 3 rows of afghan stitch along each side edge of afghan.

Fringe: Cut off-white in 8″ lengths. Knot 3 strands tog in first st at bottom of afghan. (Sk next st, knot 3 strands tog in next st) twice—3 fringes. With separate strand, tie fringes tog at back ½″ below knots. * Sk 7 spaces on edge, knot 3 fringes 1 st apart in spaces between sts. Tie fringes tog. Repeat from * across. Work same fringe across top edge of afghan.

Playful Kittens Afghan

The engaging kittens on this easy-to-make picture afghan are made by sewing together little one-color and two-color diagonal squares. The dimensions are especially proportioned for a small fry's bed.

ONE-COLOR SQUARES

COLOR	NUMBER NEEDED
Blue	350
Green	7
Orange	10
Amber	50
Red	8
Yellow	6
White	41
Black	5
Steel Gray	4
Lt. Gold	41

TWO-COLOR SQUARES

COLORS	NUMBER NEEDED
Lt. Gold/Amber	1
Blue/Lt. Gold	4
Blue/White	14
Blue/Black	1
Blue/Red	6
Blue/Amber	14
Blue/Orange	8
Blue/Yellow	4
Blue/Green	5
Blue/Steel Gray	2
Amber/White	1
Orange/White	1
Orange/Amber	7
Orange/Green	1
Yellow/Green	1
Yellow/Red	1
Black/White	5
Steel Gray/White	2

COLOR KEY

Symbol	Color
(white)	White
(lt. gold)	Lt. Gold
(blue)	Blue
(amber)	Amber
1	Black
2	Green
3	Orange
4	Red
5	Yellow
6	Steel Gray
7	Lt. Gold/Amber
8	Blue/Lt. Gold
9	Blue/White
10	Blue/Black
11	Blue/Red
12	Blue/Orange
13	Blue/Yellow
14	Blue/Green
15	Blue/Steel Gray
16	Amber/White
17	Orange/Green
18	Orange/White
19	Orange/Amber
20	Yellow/Green
21	Yellow/Red
22	Black/White
23	Steel Gray/White
24	Amber/Blue

SIZE: 45″ × 68″.

MATERIALS: Worsted weight yarn, in 4-ounce skeins: 9 skeins blue; 1 skein each of green, orange, red, yellow, black, steel gray, light gold; 2 skeins each of amber, white. Aluminum crochet hook size G.

GAUGE: 1 square = 2¼″. (To test gauge, see page 108.)

GENERAL DIRECTIONS: Afghan is made up of one-color and two-color diagonal squares.

ONE-COLOR SQUARE:

Rnd 1 (wrong side): Ch 4, sl st in first ch to form ring. Ch 3, 2 dc in ring; (ch 2, 3 dc in ring) 3 times, ch 2, sl st in top of ch 3. Turn work.

Rnd 2: (right side): 2 sl sts into ch-2 sp, ch 3, 2 dc in same sp, * ch 1, (3 dc, ch 2, 3 dc) in next sp, repeat from * twice, ch 1, 3 dc in next sp over the 2 sl sts, ch 2, sl st in top of ch 3. End off; leave 8″ end for sewing.

TWO-COLOR DIAGONAL SQUARE:

Rnd 1 (wrong side): With Color A, ch 4, sl st in first ch to form ring. Ch 3, 2 dc in ring, ch 2, 3 dc in ring; drop A, draw Color B through lp on hook; with B, ch 1, 3 dc in ring, ch 2, 3 dc in ring, ch 2, sl st in top of ch 3. Turn work.

Rnd 2 (right side): 2 sl sts into ch-2 sp, ch 3, 2 dc in same sp, ch 1, (3 dc, ch 2, 3 dc) in next sp, ch 1, 3 dc in next sp, ch 2, drop B; with A, 3 dc in same sp, ch 1, (3 dc, ch 2, 3 dc) in next sp, ch 1, 3 dc in next sp over the 2

sl sts, ch 2, sl st in top of ch 3. End off A and B; leave 8″ ends for sewing.

JOINING: Hold 2 squares with right sides tog, positioned (when possible) so yarn end for sewing is in upper right-hand corner. Thread yarn in tapestry needle. Matching sts on front and back squares, sew with overcast st in outer lps only across side, beg and ending with one corner st. When a yarn end is not available, sew with matching yarn. Join squares in rows across, then sew rows tog, or join squares to form parts of design, then sew these units tog. Be sure all 4-corner junctions are firmly joined. Weave in all yarn ends. Steam-press lightly, if needed.

AFGHAN: Following General Directions, make one-color and two-color diagonal squares in the amount given with the chart; sew them tog as directed in Joining, following chart.

APPLIQUÉ DETAILS:

Nose and Mouth (make 2): With black, ch 10″. Weave in yarn ends. Position as shown in color photograph, wrong side of ch up. Sew in place with matching sewing thread.

Eyes (make 4): With green, ch 4. Join with sl st to form ring. Ch 2, 6 dc in ring; sl st in top of ch 2. End off. Weave in yarn ends. With black, make four 2½″ chains; end off. Weave in yarn ends. Position black chains and green eyes as shown in photograph. Sew in place with matching sewing threads.

Yarn Ends: With red, ch 16″. With yellow, ch 14″. Weave in yarn ends. Position as shown in photograph, with right side of chain up. Sew in place with matching sewing threads.

Afghans to Knit

Rose Afghan Set

A rose is a rose is a rose—unless, of course, it's an afghan. An unusually luxurious afghan and pillow set, this features diamonds, marked off with popcorn puffs, and roses embroidered in the challenging bullion stitch.

Afghan

SIZE: 56″ × 48″, plus fringe.

MATERIALS: Knitting worsted weight yarn, 15 4-ounce skeins white (W). For embroidery (afghan and pillow): 1 skein each of scarlet, blue, kelly green. Knitting needles No. 13. Crocket hook size I. Tapestry needle.

GAUGE: 11 sts = 4″; 4 rows = 1″ (double strand of yarn). (To test gauge, see page 111.)

Note: Popcorn: K very loosely in front and back of 1 st until there are 5 sts in 1 st, sl st worked in off left-hand needle, (with left-hand needle, pass 2nd st from tip of right-hand needle over and off needle) 4 times (1 st of group left).

AFGHAN: Panels 1, 3 and 5: With double strand of W, cast on 29 sts. K 1 row, p 1 row.

Row 3: (right side): K 14, popcorn in next st (see Note), k 14.

Row 4: P 13, k 3, p 13.

Row 5: K 13, p 3, k 13.

Row 6: P 12, k 5, p 12.

Row 7: K 12, p 5, k 12.

Row 8: P 11, k 7, p 11.

Row 9: K 10, popcorn in next st, p 7, popcorn in next st, k 10.

Row 10: P 9, k 11, p 9.

Row 11: K 9, p 11, k 9.

Row 12: P 8, k 13, p 8.

Row 13: K 8, p 13, k 8.

Row 14: P 7, k 15, p 7.

Row 15: K 6, popcorn in next st, p 15, popcorn in next st, k 6.

Row 16: P 5, k 19, p 5.

Row 17: K 5, p 19, k 5.

Row 18: P 4, k 21, p 4.

Row 19: K 4, p 21, k 4.

Row 20: P 1, k 1, p 1, k 23, p 1, k 1, p 1.

Row 21: K 1, p 1, popcorn in next st, p 23, popcorn in next st, p 1, k 1.

Rows 22–39: Working back from row 20, work in pat to row 3. Repeat rows 4–39, 5 times more—6 diamonds in all. P 1 row, k 1 row. Bind off in p.

Panels 2 and 4: With double strand of W, cast on 23 sts, K 1 row, p 1 row.

Row 3: (right side): K 11, popcorn in next st, k 11.

Row 4: P 10, k 3, p 10.

Row 5: K 10, p 3, k 10.

Row 6: P 9, k 5, p 9.

Row 7: K 9, p 5, k 9.

Row 8: P 8, k 7, p 8.

Row 9: K 7, popcorn in next st, p 7, popcorn in next st, k 7.

Row 10: P 6, k 11, p 6.

Row 11: K 6, p 11, k 6.

Row 12: P 5, k 13, p 5.

Row 13: K 5, p 13, k 5.

Row 14: P 4, k 15, p 4.

Row 15: K 3, popcorn in next st, p 15, popcorn in next st, k 3.

Row 16: P 2, k 19, p 2.

Row 17: K 2, p 19, k 2.

Row 18: P 1, k 21, p 1.

Row 19: K 1, p 21, k 1.

Row 20: Knit.

Row 21: Purl.

Rows 22–39: Working back from row 20, work in pat to row 3. Repeat rows 4–39, 5 times more—6 diamonds in all. P 1 row, k 1 row. Bind off in p.

FINISHING: Steam-press panels. Embroider scarlet roses in center of purl diamonds as follows:

   With double strand of scarlet, embroider 8

bullion stitches in a radiating circle. With single strand of green, embroider outline stitch stems. With triple strand of green, embroider straight stitch leaves (see Stitch Details, page 103). With backstitch, sew the 5 panels together in proper sequence, then embroider blue bullion stitch roses as for scarlet roses in center of knit diamonds.

With double strand of W, work a row of sc on each long edge, keeping work flat.

Fringe: Cut strands of W 22″ long. Using 6 strands for each fringe, pull through every 4th st on cast-on and bound-off edges. Knot ends of yarn close to edge of afghan. Trim.

Pillow

SIZE: 20″ square.

MATERIALS: Knitting worsted weight yarn, 2 4-ounce skeins white. Knitting needles No. 10. For embroidery: See under Afghan, Materials. 20″ square pillow form, or stuffing. Tapestry needle.

GAUGE: 15 sts = 4″. 11 rows = 2″.

PILLOW: FRONT: Cast on 75 sts. K 1 row, p 1 row.

Row 3: K 13, popcorn in next st (see Note under Afghan), (k 23, popcorn in next st) twice, k 13.

Row 4: P 12, (k 3, p 21) twice, k 3, p 12.

Row 5: K 12, (p 3, k 21) twice, p 3, k 12.

Row 6: P 11, (k 5, p 19) twice, k 5, p 11.

Row 7: K 11, (p 5, k 19) twice, p 5, k 11.

Row 8: P 10, (k 7, p 17) twice, k 7, p 10.

Row 9: K 9, (popcorn in next st, p 7, popcorn in next st, k 15) twice, popcorn in next st, p 7, popcorn in next st, k 9.

Row 10: P 8, (k 11, p 13) twice, k 11, p 8.

Row 11: K 8, (p 11, k 13) twice, p 11, k 8.

Row 12: P 7, (k 13, p 11) twice, k 13, p 7.

Row 13: K 7, (p 13, k 11) twice, p 13, k 7.

Row 14: P 6, (k 15, p 9) twice, k 15, p 6.

Row 15: K 5, (popcorn in next st, p 15, popcorn in next st, k 7) twice, popcorn in next st, p 15, popcorn in next st, k 5.

Row 16: P 4, (k 19, p 5) twice, k 19, p 4.

Row 17: K 4, (p 19, k 5) twice, p 19, k 4.

Row 18: P 3, (k 21, p 3) 3 times.

Row 19: K 3, (p 21, k 3) 3 times.

Row 20: P 2, (k 23, p 1) twice, k 23, p 2.

Row 21: K 1, (popcorn in next st, p 23) 3 times, popcorn in next st, k 1.

Rows 22–39: Working back from row 20, work in pat to row 3. Repeat rows 4–39 twice more. P 1 row. Bind off.

BACK: Cast on 75 sts. Work in stockinette st (k 1 row, p 1 row) until piece measures same length as front. Bind off.

FINISHING: Steam-press to measure 20″ square. Embroider front as for afghan. Sew three sides, insert pillow (or stuffing), close fourth side.

Firelight Afghan

Bright as a flame and just as warm, this spectacular afghan is knit in Nordic patterns with double strands of yarn—all in one piece.

SIZE: 54″ × 68″.

MATERIALS: Knitting worsted weight yarn, 4-ounce skeins: 8 skeins mulberry (M), 6 skeins bright watermelon (W), 4 skeins each of flame (F) and navy (N), 2 skeins lilac (L). Circular knitting needle, 36″ length, No. 11.

GAUGE: 7 sts = 2″, 4 rows = 1″ (double strand). (To test gauge, see page 111.)

AFGHAN: Beg at bottom border, with 2 strands of M held tog, cast on 185 sts.

Row 1: (wrong side): K across.

Row 2: K 2 tog, k to last 2 sts, k 2 tog.

Row 3: K across.

Rows 4–9: Repeat rows 2 and 3, 3 times— 177 sts. Cut M; join 2 strands of W.

Notes: Use 2 strands throughout; cut and join colors as needed. When using 2 colors in one row, carry unused color loosely across wrong side.

Rows 10–53: Following chart, work in stockinette st (k 1 row, p 1 row). On k rows repeat from A to B across to last 9 sts, work from A to C. On p rows, work from C to A, repeat from B to A across.

Repeat rows 10–53, 4 times more (5 times in all), then repeat rows 10–47 once.

Top Border: With M, k across.

Next Row: Inc in first st, k across, inc in last st. K 1 row even. Repeat last 2 rows 3 times— 185 sts. Bind off loosely.

SIDE BORDERS: From right side, with M, pick up and k 224 sts evenly spaced along side edge (mark side edge into 8 equal parts; pick up 28 sts in each section). Work as for top border—232 sts. Bind off.

FINISHING: Run in all yarn ends on wrong side. Weave borders tog at corners.

|N| Navy

|S| Lilac

|●| Mulberry

|/| Brt. Watermelon

|X| Flame

Row 53

Row 47

Row 10

B   C   A

Argyle Afghan

This bonnie pattern from the highlands of Scotland has alternating panels of sporty argyle and cable-and-garter stitch. It's ideal for the preppy set.

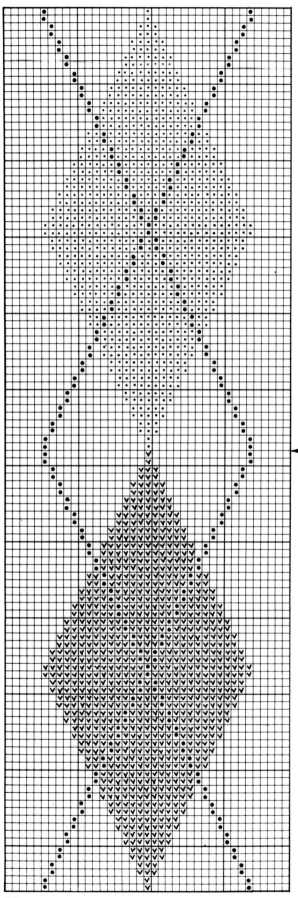

SIZE: About 50″ × 70″, plus fringe.

MATERIALS: Knitting worsted weight yarn, 9 4-ounce balls hunter green, main color (MC), 1 ball each of kelly green (A), black (B), and yellow (C). Knitting needles No. 10 (6 mm). Cable stitch needle. Six bobbins.

GAUGE: 4 sts = 1″; 11 rows = 2″. (To test gauge, see page 111.)

Notes: Use a bobbin for each color change, except where the color is used again after 1 or 2 sts of another color. In this case, the color may be carried loosely across back of work. When changing colors, always hold the color which has just been worked to the left and pick up the new color from underneath. This twists colors so that there are no holes.

ARGYLE PANEL (make 3): With MC, cast on 39 sts.

Row 1: K 5, put a marker on needle, k 29, put a marker on needle, k 5.

Row 2: K 5, sl marker, p 29, sl marker, k 5.
   Keeping 5 sts each end of needle in garter st and remaining sts in stockinette st, following chart, work from bottom to top of chart 3 times, then repeat first half of chart to arrow.

Last 2 Rows: With MC, work as for first 2 rows. Bind off.

CABLE PATTERN STITCH:

Row 1: K 1, p 2, k 4, p 2, k 5, p 2, k 4, p 2, k 1.

Row 2: P 1, k 2, p 4, k 2, p 1, k 3, p 1, k 2, p 4, k 2, p 1.

Row 3: K 1, p 2, sl next 2 sts onto cable needle and hold in back of work, k next 2 sts, k 2 sts from cable needle (cable 4), p 2, k 5, p 2, cable 4, p 2, k 1.

Row 4: Repeat row 2.

☐　**MC**

☑　**A**

⊡　**B**

◉　**C**

Row 5: Repeat row 1.

Row 6: Repeat row 2.
Repeat these 6 rows for cable pattern st.

LEFT CABLE PANEL: With MC, cast on 31 sts.

Row 1: K 1, put a marker on needle, work row 1 of cable pattern st on next 23 sts, put a marker on needle, k 7.

Row 2: K 7, sl marker, work row 2 of cable pattern st on next 23 sts, sl marker, k 1.
   Keeping 23 sts between markers in cable pattern st and remaining sts in garter st, work even until pattern st has been worked 68 times. Bind off.

RIGHT CABLE PANEL: With MC, cast on 31 sts.

Row 1: K 7, put a marker on needle, work row 1 of cable pattern st on next 23 sts, put a marker on needle, k 1.

Row 2: K 1, sl marker, work row 2 of cable pattern st on next 23 sts, sl marker, k 7.

   Keeping 23 sts between markers in cable pattern st and remaining sts in garter st, work even until pattern st has been worked 68 times. Bind off.

CENTER CABLE PANEL (make 2): With MC, cast on 25 sts.

Row 1: K 1, put a marker on needle, work row 1 of cable pattern st on next 23 sts, put a marker on needle, k 1.

Row 2: K 1, sl marker, work row 2 of cable pattern st on next 23 sts, sl marker, k 1.
   Keeping 23 sts between markers in cable pattern st and remaining sts in garter st, work even until cable pattern st has been worked 68 times. Bind off.

FINISHING: With MC, sew panels tog as follows: right cable panel, argyle panel, center cable panel, argyle panel, center cable panel, argyle panel, left cable panel.

Fringe: Cut MC strands 10″ long. Knot 2 strands in every 3rd st across each short end of afghan. Trim fringe evenly.

Inishmore Afghan

Ten textured pattern stitches borrowed from Irish sweaters are worked in squares, alternating with plain squares, to lend textural variety to this handsome afghan.

SIZE: About 52″ × 60″, without fringe.

MATERIALS: Knitting worsted weight yarn, 3½-ounce ball, 10 balls off-white. Knitting needles No. 8. One dp needle. Aluminum crochet hook size H.

GAUGE: 9 sts = 2″. (To test gauge, see page 111.)

PATTERN 1 (Bobble Pat—17 sts):

Row 1: (right side): * K 1, p 1, repeat from *, end k 1.

Row 2: Purl.

Row 3: * Bobble st (k 4 sts in 1 st, alternating from front to back. Turn, p these 4 sts. Turn, sl 1, k 3 tog, pass sl st over last st), p 1, k 1, p 1, repeat from *, end bobble st—5 bobbles.

Row 4: Repeat row 2.

Row 5: Repeat row 1.

Row 6: Repeat row 2.

Row 7: * K 1, p 1, bobble st, p 1, repeat from *, end p 1, k 1–4 bobbles.

Row 8: Repeat row 2. Repeat these 8 rows for pat 1.

PATTERN 2 (Diagonal Left—17 sts):

Row 1 (right side): P 1, (k 3, p 3) twice, k 3, p 1.

Row 2: (P 3, k 3) twice, p 3, k 2.

Row 3: Repeat row 2.

Row 4: Repeat row 1.

Row 5: K 2, (p 3, k 3) twice, p 3.

Row 6: Repeat row 5. Repeat these 6 rows for pat 2.

PATTERN 3 (Diagonal Right—17 sts):

Row 1: (right side): P 1, (k 3, p 3) twice, k 3, p 1.

Row 2: K 2, (p 3, k 3) twice, p 3.

Row 3: Repeat row 2.

Row 4: Repeat row 1.

Row 5: (P 3, k 3) twice, p 3, k 2.

Row 6: Repeat row 5. Repeat these 6 rows for pat 3.

PATTERN 4 (Box St—17 sts):

Row 1: (right side): K 1, (p 3, k 3) twice, p 3, k 1.

Row 2: P 1, (k 3, p 3) twice, k 3, p 1.

Rows 3 and 4: Repeat row 1.

Row 5: Repeat row 2.

Row 6: Repeat row 1. Repeat these 6 rows for pat 4.

PATTERN 5 (Seed and Cable—17 sts):

Row 1: (right side): P 1, (k 3, p 1, k 1, p 1) twice, k 3, p 1.

Row 2: (P 5, k 1) twice, p 5.

Row 3: P 1, (sk 2 sts, k next st, k the 2 skipped sts, sl knitted st already worked off needle, p 1, k 1, p 1) twice, sk 2 sts, k next st, k the 2 skipped sts, sl knitted st already worked off needle (cable twist—CT), p 1.

Row 4: Repeat row 2.

Row 5: Repeat row 1.

Row 6: Repeat row 2. Repeat rows 3–6 for pat 5.

PATTERN 6 (Seed St—17 sts):

Row 1: (K 1, p 1) 8 times, k 1.

Row 2: (P 1, k 1) 8 times, p 1.

Row 3: Repeat row 2.

Row 4: Repeat row 1. Repeat these 4 rows for pat 6.

PATTERN 7 (Raised Diagonal Right—17 sts):

Row 1: * K 2, sk 1 st, insert needle as to p in next st, turn and k the skipped st, take the 2 sts off left-hand needle (2 twist right or 2 TR), repeat from *, end k 1.

Row 2 and All Even Rows: Purl.

Row 3: K 1, (2 TR, k 2) 4 times.

Row 5: (2 TR, k 2) 4 times, end last repeat, k 3.

LEFT CABLE (LC—12 sts): Work as for RC, but on cable twist, sl 4 to dp needle, hold in front of work, k 4, k 4 from dp needle.

STRIP 1: Cast on 77 sts.

Row 1: Work 12 sts RC (see Right Cable), k 53, work last 12 sts RC. Repeat row 1 for 15 times more (garter st border, RC each side). The 12-st RC will be worked each end for entire strip.

BOX A: Row 1: Work RC, k 17, sl 1 with yarn in back, 17 sts pat 1, sl 1 with yarn in back, k 17, work RC.

Row 2: RC, p 17, p the sl st, 17 sts pat 1, p the sl st, p 17, RC. Repeat rows 1 and 2 until there are 20 rows.

Row 21: RC, 17 sts pat 3, sl 1 with yarn in back, k 17, sl 1, 17 sts pat 2, RC.

Row 22: RC, 17 sts pat 2, p the sl st, p 17, p the sl st, 17 sts pat 3, RC. Repeat rows 21 and 22 until there are 20 rows in this group of boxes.

Rows 41–60: Repeat rows 1 and 2. See diagram, Box A.

BOX B: K 16 rows garter st (k each row) with RC at each end as established.

Row 1: RC, k 17, sl 1, 17 sts pat 9, sl 1, k 17, RC.

Row 2: Rc, p 17, p the sl st, 17 sts pat 9, p the sl st, p 17, RC. Repeat rows 1 and 2 until there are 20 rows.

Row 21: RC, 17 sts pat 10, sl 1, k 17, sl 1, 17 sts pat 10, RC.

Row 22: RC, 17 sts pat 10, p the sl st, p 17, p the sl st, 17 sts pat 10, RC. Repeat rows 21 and 22 until there are 20 rows in this group of boxes.

Rows 41–60: Repeat rows 1 and 2. See diagram, Box B.

BOX C: K 16 rows garter st with RC at each end.

Row 1: Rc, k 17, sl 1, 17 sts pat 8, sl 1, k 17, RC.

Row 2: RC, p 17, p the sl st, 17 sts pat 8, p the sl st, p 17, RC. Repeat rows 1 and 2 until there are 20 rows.

Row 21: RC, 17 sts pat 6, sl 1, k 17, sl 1, 17 sts pat 6, RC.

Row 22: RC, 17 sts pat 6, p the sl st, p 17, p the sl st, 17 sts pat 6, RC. Repeat rows 21 and 22 until there are 20 rows in this group of boxes.

Rows 41–60: Repeat rows 1 and 2, working pat 7 instead of 8 so diagonal goes in opposite direction. See diagram, Box C.

BOX D: K 16 rows garter st with RC at each end.

Row 1: RC, k 17, sl 1, 17 sts pat 4, sl 1, k 17, RC.

Row 2: RC, p 17, p sl st, 17 sts pat 4, p sl st, p 17, RC. Repeat rows 1 and 2 until there are 20 rows.

Row 21: RC, 17 sts pat 5, sl 1, k 17, sl 1, 17 sts pat 5, RC.

Row 22: RC, 17 sts pat 5, p sl st, p 17, p sl st, 17 sts pat 5, RC. Repeat rows 21 and 22 until there are 20 rows in this group of boxes.

Rows 41–60: Repeat rows 1 and 2. See diagram, Box D.

BOX E: K 16 rows garter st with RC at each end as established. Work as for Box A. K 16 rows garter st with RC at each end. Bind off.

STRIP 2: See diagram.

STRIP 3: Work same as for Strip 1, working 12 Left Cable sts each side of strip, instead of Right Cable each side.

FINISHING: Wet block each strip if necessary. Wet with cold water, lay on a towel to measurements. Dry away from heat and sun. Weave Strip 2 to one side of Strips 1 and 3. From right side, sl st along each side edge, making sure work lies flat. For fringe, cut 12" strands. Knot 4 strands tog in end st at bottom edge and in every 3rd st across. Repeat fringe on top edge.

Lilliputian Coverlets

For crib or bassinet: two baby-size afghans to make for gift-giving. One to knit—a leaf coverlet in yellow and white. One to crochet—two favorite patterns combined, granny squares and ripples.

Leaf Coverlet

SIZE: 29″ × 40″.

MATERIALS: Knitting worsted weight yarn, 3 3½-ounce skeins each of yellow and white. Knitting needles No. 8 (5 mm). Crochet hook size I or 9 (5½ mm). Yarn needle.

GAUGE: Each small square should measure about 6″ square. (To test gauge, see page 111.)

SMALL SQUARE (make 24): With white, cast on 3 sts.

Row 1 (wrong side): Knit.

Row 2: K 1, (yo, k 1) twice—5 sts.

Row 3: K 1, p 3, k 1.

Row 4: K 1, (yo, k 1) 4 times—9 sts.

Row 5: K 2, p 5, k 2.

Row 6: K 1, yo, k 3, yo, k 1, yo, k 3, yo, k 1–13 sts.

Row 7: K 3, p 7, k 3.

Row 8: K 1, yo, k 5, yo, k 1, yo, k 5, yo, k 1–17 sts.

Row 9: K 4, p 9, k 4.

Row 10: K 1, yo, k 7, yo, k 1, yo, k 7, yo, k 1—21 sts.

Row 11: K 5, p 11, k 5.

Row 12: K 1, yo, k 9, yo, k 1, yo, k 9, yo, k 1—25 sts.

Row 13: K 6, p 13, k 6.

Row 14: K 1, yo, k 11, yo, k 1, yo, k 11, yo, k 1—29 sts.

Row 15: K 7, p 15, k 7.

Row 16: K 1, yo, k 13, yo, k 1, yo, k 13, yo, k 1—33 sts.

Row 17: K 8, p 17, k 8.

Row 18: K 1, yo, k 7, k 2 tog, k 13, k 2 tog, k 7, yo, k 1—33 sts.

Row 19: K 9, p 15, k 9.

Row 20: K 1, yo, k 8, k 2 tog, k 11, k 2 tog, k 8, yo, k 1—33 sts.

Row 21: K 10, p 13, k 10.

Row 22: K 1, yo, k 9, k 2 tog, k 9, k 2 tog, k 9, yo, k 1—33 sts.

Row 23: K 11, p 11, k 11.

Row 24: K 1, yo, k 10, k 2 tog, k 7, k 2 tog, k 10, yo, k 1—33 sts.

Row 25: K 12, p 9, k 12.

Row 26: K 1, yo, k 11, k 2 tog, k 5, k 2 tog, k 11, yo, k 1—33 sts.

Row 27: K 13, p 7, k 13.

Row 28: K 1, yo, k 12, k 2 tog, k 3, k 2 tog, k 12, yo, k 1—33 sts.

Row 29: K 14, p 5, k 14.

Row 30: K 1, yo, k 13, k 2 tog, k 1, k 2 tog, k 13, yo, k 1—33 sts.

Row 31: K 15, p 3, k 15.

Row 32: K 1, yo, k 14, k 3 tog, k 14, yo, k 1—33 sts.

Row 33: Knit.

Row 34: K 1, yo, k to within last st, end yo, k 1—35 sts.

Row 35: Knit.

Rows 36–39: Repeat rows 34 and 35 twice—39 sts. Cut white; join yellow.

Row 40: With yellow, k across, dec 1 st each side—37 sts.

Row 41: Purl.

Row 42: Repeat row 40—35 sts.

Row 43: Knit.

Row 44: Purl, dec 1 st each side—33 sts.

Row 45: Knit. Repeat rows 40–45 until 3 sts remain. K 3 tog. End off.

FINISHING: Arrange 4 small squares to form a large square, as shown on chart. From right side, with care to have rows matching and seams elastic, with matching color yarn, sew from outer edge to center through knots at ends of adjacent rows. Close center by inserting needle under center st in first row of each petal and drawing sts tog. End off. Arrange squares as illustrated, having 2 squares in width, 3 squares in length. From right side, matching patterns and keeping seams elastic, sew large squares tog.

Edging: From right side, with yellow, work 1 rnd sc around entire edge, working 3 sc in

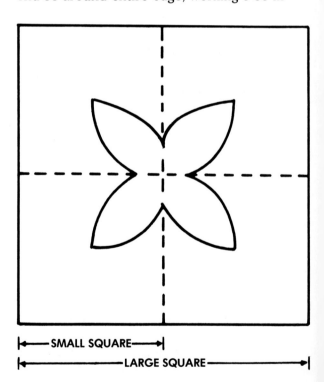

SMALL SQUARE

LARGE SQUARE

each corner; join with a sl st in first sc. Ch 1; do not turn.

Rnds 2–4: Sc in each sc around, working 3 sc in each corner. Join with a sl st in first sc. Ch 1; do not turn. Repeating rnd 2, work 1 rnd white, 4 rnds yellow, 1 rnd white.

Next Rnd (picot rnd): * Sc in each of next 3 sc, ch 3, sc in 3rd ch from hook, repeat from * around. Join; end off.

Granny Ripple Baby Afghan

SIZE: 32" × 48".

MATERIALS: Knitting worsted weight yarn, 2 4-ounce skeins each of white, yellow and mint green. Crochet hooks sizes G and J or 6 and 10 (4¼ mm and 6 mm). Yarn needle.

GAUGE: Granny square = 2¼" (size G hook). 4 sc = 1" (size J hook).

AFGHAN: GRANNY SQUARE: With yellow, ch 6. Sl st in first ch to form ring.

Rnd 1: Ch 3 (counts as 1 dc), 2 dc in ring, (ch 3, 3 dc in ring) 3 times, ch 3, sl st in top of ch 3 at beg of rnd. End off.

Rnd 2: Join green with a sl st in a ch-3 sp; ch 3, 2 dc in same sp, ch 3, 3 dc in same sp, (ch 1, 3 dc, ch 3, 3 dc in next sp) 3 times, ch 1, join with a sl st in top of ch 3. End off.

CENTER: Join 5 granny squares in a row in this way: Work 2nd square through rnd 1.

Next Rnd: Join green with a sl st in a ch-3 sp; ch 3, 2 dc in same sp, ch 1, drop lp off hook; insert hook through ch-3 lp of previous square, pull dropped lp through ch 1; pull tight, work 3 more dc in corner and finish square. Join 3 more squares to previous square in same way to make center row, squares 1–5 on diagram.

Join 4 squares to each side of the 5 squares, setting them into the notches between the squares in this way: Work square through rnd 1.

Next Rnd: Join green with a sl st in a ch-3 sp; ch 3, 2 dc in same sp, ch 1, drop lp off hook, insert hook through ch-3 lp at outer point of first square, pull dropped lp through, ch 1; pull tight; complete corner with 3 dc, drop lp off hook, insert hook in next ch-1 sp, pull dropped lp through ch 1; pull tight; join as before to joining between squares, ch 1, finish corner of new square; continue to join 2nd side of new square to next square. When joining next square, join as before to previous square and to square of center row. These are squares 6–9 and 10–13 on diagram.

Now join a square to each side of the end squares of the center row (squares 14, 15, 16, 17). These last 4 squares are joined only on one side—17 squares have been joined for center of afghan.

RIPPLE BAND:

Rnd 1 (wrong side): From wrong side, with green and size J hook, join yarn in any notch between squares on side of center piece, * work sc in back lp of each dc and ch to ch 3 at point, sc in next ch at point, ch 2, sk 1 ch, sc in next ch, sc in back lp of each dc and ch down next side, sc in back lp of first dc of next square, repeat from * around, working 8 sc on each side, ch 2 at each point. On outer edge of each end square, work sc, ch 2, sc at each outer point. At end of rnd, sl st in first sc; ch 1, turn.

Rnd 2 (right side): Sk first sc, * sc in back lp of 7 sc to point, sc in first ch, ch 2, sc in 2nd ch, sc in back lp of 7 sc to notch, sk 2 sc at notch, repeat from * around. On outer edge of each end square, work sc, ch 2, sc at each outer point, sc in back lp of each sc across— 11 sc across outer edge of each end square, 8 sc on each side of notches, ch 2 at each point. At end of rnd, sl st in first sc; ch 1, turn.

Rnd 3 (wrong side): Sk first sc, * sc in back lp of 7 sc to point, sc in first ch, ch 2, sc in 2nd ch, sc in back lp of 7 sc to notch, sk 2 sc at notch, repeat from * around. On outer edge of each end square, work sc, ch 2, sc at each outer point, sc in back lp of each sc across— 13 sc across outer edge of each end square, 8 sc on each side of notches, ch 2 at each point. Sl st in first sc; ch 1, turn.

Rnd 4: Work as for rnd 2, having 15 sc across outer edge. Cut green; turn.

Rnd 5 (wrong side): With yellow, make lp on hook; beg in any notch, sc in back lp of 2nd sc and next 6 sc, * sc in first ch at point, ch 2, sc in 2nd ch, sc in back lp of 7 sc, sk 2 sc at notch, sc in back lp of 7 sc, repeat from * around, working 2 more sc across outer edge of end squares, end sc in back lp of last 7 sc. Sl st in first sc; ch 1, turn.

Rnd 6: Work as for rnd 2.

Rnds 7 and 8: Work in ridge pat as established, working 1 rnd each of yellow and white. At end of rnd 8 there are 23 sc across outer edge of each end square.

Sk 7 sc from each end of each end square; place a marker in 8th sc in from each end. A granny square will be centered on remaining sts. With size G hook, work a granny square through rnd 1. With green, work first shell of corner of rnd 2, ch 1, drop lp off hook. With right side of afghan facing you, insert hook through both lps of marked sc, pull lp through, ch 1 tightly. (Work next 3 dc of square, drop lp off hook; sk 3 sc on afghan, insert hook through both lps of next sc, pull dropped lp through, ch 1 tightly) twice. Ch 1, finish square.

Rnd 9 (wrong side): With white and size J hook, work sc around afghan as before, working sc in back lp of each dc and ch on added squares, sc, ch 2, sc at each outer point.

Rnds 10–16: Working in ridge pat as established, work 3 rnds more of white, 4 rnds green.

GRANNY SQUARE BORDER: With size G hook, make 34 squares, joining them to each other and setting them into notches on each side. There will be 7 squares on each long side, 3 squares on each short side and 3 squares tog, side by side, across each corner. Make 4 more squares, joining to center square at each corner.

RIPPLE BORDER:

Rnd 1 (wrong side): With green and size J hook, work as for rnd 1 of ripple band.

Rnd 2 (right side): Work as for rnd 2 of ripple band.

Rnds 3–8: Working 2 rnds green, 4 rnds yellow, work as for rnds 3–8 of ripple band.

Work 4 separate granny squares, joining a square to center 9 sts as before.

Rnd 9 (wrong side): With white, work as for rnd 9 of ripple band.

Rnd 10 (right side): Work in ridge pat as established; on outer edge of 4 corner squares, work as follows: After ch 2 at corner, sc in 2nd ch of previous rnd, sc in back lp of next 2 sc, ch 2, sk next sc, sc in back lp of next 3 sc, ch 2, sc in back lp of each of next 2 sc, sc in corner ch, ch 2, continue in pat around.

Rnd 11: Work in ridge pat as established; on outer edge of 4 corner squares, work as follows: After ch 2 at corner, (sc in 2nd ch of previous rnd, sc in back lp of next sc, sk next sc, sc in back lp of next sc, sc in next ch, ch 2) 3 times.

Rnd 12: Work in ridge pat. On ch 2 increase at each corner of coverlet, work sc in first ch, ch 2, sc in 2nd ch.

Rnd 13: Work in ridge pat. On each corner of coverlet work as follows: * After ch 2 at corner, sc in 2nd ch of previous rnd, sc in back lp of next 2 sc, sk next 2 sc, sc in back lp of next 2 sc, sc in next ch, ch 2 (over ch 2 of previous rnd), repeat from * twice.

Rnds 14 and 15: Work in ridge pat. On each corner of coverlet, work ch increase over each ch 2 increase.

Rnd 16: Work in ridge pat. On each corner of coverlet, work as follows: * After ch 2 at corner, sc in 2nd ch of previous rnd, sc in back lp of next 4 sc, sk next 2 sc, sc in back lp of next 4 sc, sc in next ch, ch 2, repeat from * twice.

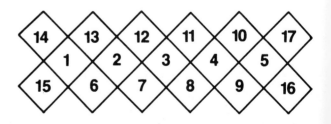

P A R T III
GENERAL DIRECTIONS

Making the Quilt Top

PATTERNS: In making a pieced (patchwork) or appliquéd quilt top, you will need a stiff pattern, also called a template, for each separate part of the design. Use thin but firm cardboard for your pattern, such as shirt lining. Some prefer heavy sandpaper, which does not slip on fabric. If the pattern is to be used many times, make duplicates and discard each as its edges become frayed from continued use.

Or, cut your pattern from sheet plastic, preferably transparent. Whatever the material, make your stiff pattern with one of the following three methods, as directed for each project: 1) Trace actual-size pattern given; glue tracing to cardboard; let dry; then cut out. 2) If our pattern is given on squares, you must enlarge it to its actual size. Draw a grid on a sheet of paper with the same number of squares as in our grid, but making each square of your grid the size directed (usually 1″); the grid can be easily drawn on graph paper. Or, if graph paper is not available, on plain paper mark dots around the edges 1″ apart (or the size directed) and form the grid by joining the dots across opposite sides of the paper. Then copy design onto your grid, square by square. Glue to cardboard and cut on lines of design, ignoring the grid lines. An easier procedure is to have the design enlarged by photostat, if such a service is available in your area. 3) For very simple geometric shapes, such as squares, rectangles, and circles, you simply make the pattern yourself, following dimensions given.

It is essential that patch patterns be accurate. If the patterns are not perfect, neither will be the patches, and they may be impossible to piece together properly. To aid in making good patterns, you should have good tools, made of metal or plastic: a ruler with a perfect edge, a triangle, a T-square, and a compass. After you have made your patterns, test their accuracy before cutting any patches. If there is a Piecing Diagram, fit patterns together as shown or draw around them on paper. If piecing a large eight-pointed star with diamond patches, place (or draw) eight diamonds together with points meeting in center, to create a small eight-pointed star; there should be no gaps between or overlapping of the diamond segments. If making a design entirely from hexagons, make sure that six hexagons will fit neatly around the six sides of a center hexagon.

Window Templates: Our patterns are made the size of the finished patch piece, that is, what shows when the quilt top is assembled. The seam allowance is not included in the pattern, but is added when patches are cut. If you wish to cut your seam allowance with perfectly even edges, you may want to make a

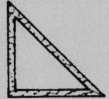

Window Templates

window template. Draw pattern shape as before, then draw another line around it exactly ¼″ away. Cut on both lines, leaving a frame. The window template is more difficult and time consuming to make, but it will make patches easier to cut. It is also advisable for using with certain prints, when placement of motifs is important.

PATCH PIECES: Use fabrics that are closely woven, so seams will hold and edges will not fray. The fabric should be fairly soft, but should not be so thin that seam allowances will show through. Before cutting patches, wash new fabrics to preshrink and remove sizing. Wash scraps in a net bag. Press all fabrics smooth. Lay fabric out flat, wrong side up for patch pieces. (See below for how to cut appliqué pieces.) Lay pattern on fabric, placing it so as many straight sides of pattern as possible are with the crosswise and lengthwise grain of fabric. If necessary, pull threads in both directions to determine grain. Using a sharp, hard pencil (light-colored for dark fabrics, dark-colored for light fabrics), draw around pattern; hold pencil at an outward angle, so that point is firmly against edge of pattern. Reposition pattern ½″ away and draw around as before. Continue marking patterns ½″ apart; do not cut fabric until all the patterns of one color are marked.

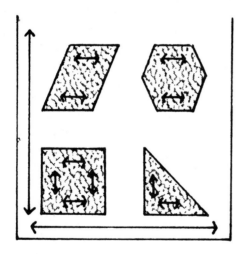

Straight Edges with Grain

Note: If large border pieces are to be cut later from the same fabric, be sure to consider their dimensions when marking smaller pieces; you may wish to mark your patches in vertical rows. Do not, however, cut out the border pieces before cutting patches.

When all patches of one color have been marked, cut out each patch, ¼″ away from marked line, which will be the stitching line. Cut the ¼″ seam allowance as accurately as you can, to make piecing easier. To keep patches of same shape and color together, put them in a pile and run a thread through center with a knot in one end; lift off each patch as needed.

PIECING: Several patch pieces will be joined to create a new unit, such as a larger patch or a block. Before sewing, lay out all pieces needed for the block. Begin by joining smallest pieces first, then joining the larger pieces made into rows, then joining rows for completed block.

By Hand: You will find it easier to join small patch pieces by hand. Hand piecing is also advised for patches with curves and sharp angles.

To join two patch pieces, place them together, right sides facing. If pieces are very small, hold firmly to sew. Larger pieces can be pin-basted, matching angles first, then marked lines between. Pin curved pieces together from center out to each corner. For piecing, use #7 to #10 sharp needle, threaded with an 18″ length of mercerized cotton or cotton-wrapped polyester thread. Begin with a small knot, then stitch along marked seam line with tiny running stitches, ending with a few backstitches; if seam is long, take a tiny backstitch every few stitches. Try to make 8 to 10 running stitches per inch, evenly spaced. If thread tends to knot or fray as you sew, run it over a cake of beeswax. If sewing two bias edges together, keep thread just taut enough to prevent fabric from stretching. As you join pieces, press seams to one side, unless otherwise indicated; open seams tend to weaken construction. Try to press seams all in the same direction, although darker fabrics should not fall under lighter ones, lest they show through. As you piece and press, clip into seams of curves and other pieces where necessary, so they will lie flat. Clip away excess fabric, to avoid bunching. Be sure a seam is pressed flat before you cross it with another; take a small backstitch over the crossing.

Joining Diamonds: Diamonds may be pieced together in same manner as for other patches. When joining diamonds to form a row, stitch patches together along sides cut on straight of goods. Stitch from the wide-angled corner toward the pointed end. Trim seam at points as you piece. If piecing a star design, join the rows together to make a diamond-shaped section, matching corners carefully. When joining rows, you will be stitching along the bias edges; keep thread slightly taut.

However, it may prove difficult when piecing diamonds to keep angles sharp and seams precise. If so, prepare a paper liner for each diamond as follows: Cut a firm paper pattern from wrapping or shelf paper the exact size of cardboard pattern. Fit paper liner within pencil outline on wrong side of patch. Hold patch with liner uppermost. Fold seam allowance over each side, and tack to the paper with one stitch on each side, allowing the thread to cross corners; finish by taking an extra stitch on the first side. Cut thread; leaving about ¼". To make removal of tacking easier, do not knot thread or make any backstitches. Press lightly. Hold prepared patches right sides together, matching the edges to be seamed exactly. Whip together with fine, even stitches (about 16 to the inch), avoiding the paper as much as possible. The liners may remain in place until the quilt top is completed. To remove liners, snip tacking thread once on each patch and withdraw thread.

Joining Hexagons: You may find it easier to join hexagons by using a paper liner, as for diamonds. Join hexagons in circular fashion, starting with six hexagons around a center patch. Whipstitch edges together as for diamonds, backstitching where corners meet.

By Machine: Some quilts are made with larger patches and you might wish to piece them by machine. Set machine for 10 stitches to the inch, unless working with very heavy fabrics, and use needle #14. Use mercerized cotton thread # 50 or cotton-wrapped polyester. Follow the same procedures as for hand piecing: Pin-baste, stitch, clip seams, and press. You need not, however, begin and end your thread with each patch; let thread run on for a continuous chain of patches. Patches will be snipped apart and their seams anchored by cross-seams.

ASSEMBLING QUILT TOP: As you construct your quilt top, building from patches to blocks to rows of blocks to borders, etc., it is important to measure each unit as you make it. Blocks to be joined should be of equal size. It is also important to compare your measurements with those given in the directions and make any necessary adjustments in the size of following pieces. Our measurements are strictly mathematical and do not allow for the variance that may easily result from multiple piecing. For example: We may have calculated that the pieced center of a quilt top should measure 79½" on the sides and we instruct you to cut side border pieces 79½" long. If your piece measures 80", naturally you will want to cut border pieces 80" long. You may need to adjust size of lining and edging strips as well. That is why we do not recommend cutting the larger pieces of a quilt top before the smaller units are assembled.

To Miter Border Corners: Sew border pieces to quilt top, with an equal amount extending at each end, for the corners of quilt. Lay quilt top flat, right side down. Hold adjacent ends of border pieces together at corners with right sides facing. Keeping border flat, lift up inner corners and pin strips together diagonally from inner corners to outer corners; baste, then stitch on basting line. Cut off excess fabric to make ¼" seam; press seam open.

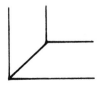

A Mitered Corner

Appliqué:

Choose a fabric that is closely woven and firm enough so a clean edge results when the pieces are cut. Press fabric smooth. There are two methods of transferring appliqué patterns to fabric:

TO TRANSFER LARGE DESIGNS: Mark a pattern on paper for each appliqué piece; do not cut out. Place paper on right side of fabric, inserting dressmaker's tracing (carbon) paper between fabric and pattern. Go over lines of pattern with tracing wheel or a dry ball-point pen, to transfer design. Remove pattern and carbon. Mark a second outline 1/4" outside design outline. Appliqué as directed below.

TO TRANSFER SMALL DESIGNS: For each motif, make a cardboard pattern: Trace design; do not cut out. Glue tracing paper to thin, stiff cardboard and let dry; cut along traced line. Place cardboard pattern on right side of fabric. Holding sharp, hard pencil at an outward angle (light-colored pencil on dark fabric and dark pencil on light fabric), mark around pattern. When marking several pieces on the same fabric, leave at least 1/2" between pieces. Mark a second outline 1/4" outside design outline. Appliqué as directed below.

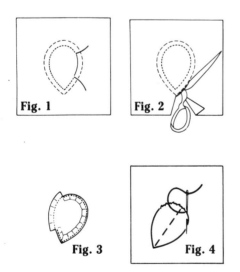

Fig. 1   Fig. 2

Fig. 3   Fig. 4

TO APPLIQUÉ BY HAND: Using matching thread and small stitches, machine-stitch all around design outline, as shown in **Fig. 1.**

This makes edge easier to turn and neater in appearance. Cut out appliqué on the outside line, as in **Fig. 2.** For a smooth edge, clip into seam allowance at curved edges and corners, then turn seam allowance to back, just inside stitching as shown in **Fig. 3,** and press.

Note: You may prefer to place some pieces so they overlap the extended seam allowance of adjacent pieces; study overall design before turning under all seam allowances.

Pin and baste the appliqués on the background, the underneath pieces first, and slip-stitch in place with tiny stitches. See **Fig. 4.**

TO APPLIQUÉ BY MACHINE: Cut out appliqués on outside lines. Pin and baste appliqués in place; do not turn under excess fabric. Straight-stitch around appliqués on marked lines. Trim away excess fabric to 1/8" from straight stitching. Set sewing machine for close zigzag stitch as directed (1/4" wide or less). Zigzag around appliqués, covering straight stitching and excess fabric.

Preparing to Quilt

LINING AND BATTING: Cut or piece lining and batting as directed. If they are to be same size as the quilt top, you may want to make them a little larger to start with, such as 1" all around, and trim after basting or quilting. For comfortable hand quilting, the lining fabric should be soft; sheets, for example, are too densely woven for the needle to pass through easily.

In planning the batting, consider the style of the quilt and its intended use. Antique quilts with their close, ornate quilting designs usually were made with only a very thin filler. If you wish to duplicate the effect, use a split layer of polyester batting. The thinner the layer of batting, the easier and finer the quilting will be. For simpler quilting designs, or where more loft or warmth is desirable, use one or two full layers of polyester batting. Polyester is generally preferable to cotton batting, as it holds together, does not lump, and will dry quickly if the quilt is washed. If using cotton batting, be sure your lines of quilting are no more than 2" apart.

BASTING: After quilting design has been marked on the quilt top, assemble top, batting, and lining: Place lining, wrong side up, on large, flat surface. Place batting on top of lining and smooth out any bumps or wrinkles. Before adding quilt top, baste batting to lining by taking two long stitches in a cross. Place quilt top on batting, right side up. Pin all layers together to hold temporarily, using large safety pins. Baste generously through all thicknesses, using a sturdy thread and a large needle. To prevent shifting, first baste on the lengthwise and crosswise grain of fabric. Then baste diagonally across in two directions and around sides, top, and bottom. If quilting is to be done with a quilting hoop or on the machine, extra care must be taken to keep basting stitches close, so they will hold in place as you work.

Quilting

BY HAND: When quilting by hand, the quilt may be stretched on a frame or in a quilting hoop. If the quilting design is especially ornate, it is best to use the frame; the hoop, on the other hand, is portable and more easily managed. If using neither hoop nor frame, you can quilt in your lap, working over a small area at a time.

Quilting Frame: Sew top and bottom edges of lining to the fabric strips attached to the long parallel bars of frame. Using strong thread so that quilt will not pull away from frame when stretched taut, sew securely with several rows of stitches. After quilt is secured in frame, start quilting midway between the long parallel bars of frame and sew toward you.

Quilting Hoop: Pull quilt taut in hoop and move any extra fullness toward the edges. Start quilting in the center and work toward edges. If necessary, cut basting thread as work progresses. As your quilting comes close to the edge, substitute smaller embroidery hoops for the larger quilting hoop, so that fabric will always remain taut.

Needle and Thread: Use a short, strong needle, between #7 and #10; experienced quilters may prefer a longer needle. If you can find it, use quilting thread, which has a silicone coating. If you can't, choose a strong (#50 to #30) cotton mercerized or a cotton-covered polyester thread. If thread knots, frays, or breaks as you quilt, try running each strand across a cake of beeswax.

Quilting Stitch: Cut 18″ strand of thread. Knot one end. Bring needle up from lining through quilt top; give a little tug to thread so that knot passes through lining only and lies buried in batting. Sew on marked line with running stitch, in two separate motions: Push needle straight down through the three layers with one hand, take needle with other hand, pull thread through and push up close to the first stitch. An experienced quilter may be able to take two or three stitches before pull thread through and push up close to the first stitch. An experienced quilter may be able to take two or three stitches before pulling needle through, holding quilt down at quilting line with thumb of the other hand; do not try this unless using a frame. Depending on thickness of fabric and batting, make stitches as small and close as you can (5 to 10 per inch); the longer the stitch, the less durable the quilting. Space stitches evenly, so

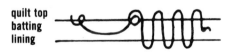

quilt top
batting
lining

Quilting Stitch

they are the same length on both sides of quilt. From time to time, look underneath to check your stitches. To end off, backstitch and take a long stitch through the top and batting only; take another backstitch and clip thread at surface; the thread end will sink into batting. If you are a beginner, practice first on a small piece in an embroidery hoop, to find the easiest and best working method for you.

Start in the middle of the quilt and stitch toward you; shift your position as you work, so that the quilting progresses fairly evenly on all sides toward the outside of the quilt.

BY MACHINE: Quilting can be done on the machine, with or without a quilting foot. When working on a machine, the best quilting patterns to use are those sewn on the diagonal or on the bias. Fabric gives a little when on the bias, making it easier to keep work flat.

As a rule, machine quilting is done with a straight stitch. Set stitch length from 6 to 12 per inch. Adjust pressure so that it is slightly heavier than for medium-weight fabrics, with the bobbin thread a little loose. If you are using a scroll or floral design, it is best to use the short open toe of the quilting foot. This allows you to follow the curved lines with ease and accuracy.

To begin, roll up half of quilt and place to right of needle. Begin stitching in center of quilt and work to the right, unrolling quilt as you go. Repeat for remaining half.

Tufting

If you wish to tuft rather than quilt, use several layers of batting between the top and lining. Mark evenly spaced points on the top surface with tailor tacks or pins. Thread a candlewick needle with candlewick yarn, or use a large-eyed needle with heavy Germantown yarn, knitting worsted, or pearl cotton. With thread double, push needle from top to lining, leaving about 5″ of thread on top. Push needle back up again to surface, about ¼″ away. Tie yarn in firm double knot. Clip ends to desired length, at least ½″. For extra strength stitch twice.

Embroidery

TO PREPARE FABRIC: To prevent fabric from raveling, bind all raw edges with masking tape, whipstitch edges by hand, or machine-stitch ⅛″ in from all edges.

FRAMES/HOOPS: Work embroidery in a frame or hoop. With the material held tautly and evenly, your stitches are more likely to be neat and accurate than if the fabric were held in hand while working.

TO BEGIN AND END A STRAND: Cut floss or yarn into 18″ strands. To begin a strand, leave an end on back and work over it to secure; to end, run needle under four or five stitches on back or take a few tiny backstitches. Do not make knots. Fasten off the thread when ending each motif, rather than carrying it to another motif.

TO REMOVE EMBROIDERY: When a mistake has been made, run a needle, eye first, under the stitches. Pull the embroidery away from the fabric; cut carefully with small scissors pressed hard against the needle. Pick out the cut portion of the embroidery and catch loose ends of the remaining stitches on back by pulling the ends under the stitches with a crochet hook.

FOR COUNTED CROSS-STITCH: For counted cross-stitch on even-weave fabrics, work stitches over a counted number of threads both horizontally and vertically, following a chart. Each symbol on the chart represents one stitch. Different symbols represent different colors.

For counted cross-stitch on gingham fabric, work stitches over checks, so that one complete cross-stitch covers one check.

When working cross-stitches, work underneath stitches in one direction and top stitches in the opposite direction, making sure all strands lie smooth and flat; allow needle to hang freely from work occasionally, to untwist floss. Make crosses touch by inserting needle in same hole used for adjacent stitch (see stitch details).

TO FINISH: When your embroidered piece is completed, finish off the back neatly by running ends into the back of the work and clipping off any excess threads. Place piece face down on a well padded surface and press, using a steam iron, or regular iron and damp pressing cloth. Press lightly from the center outward. For embroidery that is raised from the surface of the background, use extra thick, soft padding, such as a thick blanket.

STITCH DETAILS

Straight Stitch

Herringbone Stitch

Lazy Daisy Stitch

Split Stitch

French Knot

Seed Stitch

Cross-Stitch

Closed Fly Stitch

Long and Short Stitch

Couching

Chain Stitch

Blanket Stitch

Fly Stitch

Buttonhole Stitch

Running Stitch

Featherstitch

Laid Filling or
Intersected Trellis

Double Cross-Stitch

Backstitch

Turkey Work

Satin Stitch

Satin Leaf Stitch

Outline (Stem) Stitch

Padded Satin Stitch

Bullion Stitch

Woven Spider
Web Stitch

Cretan or
Open Cretan Stitch

Radiating Straight Stitch

straight, lazy daisy

straight, French knot, cross-stitch

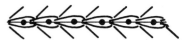

chain, straight, French knot

chain, straight, French knot

lazy daisy, straight, French knot

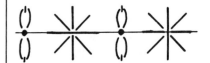

**double cross-stitch,
French knot, lazy daisy**

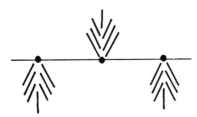

French knot, straight

**cretan, lazy daisy,
French knot, straight**

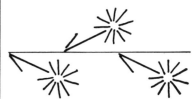

straight stitch

featherstitch, lazy daisy, straight

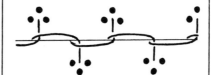

blanket, French knot

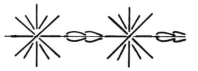

double cross-stitch, straight, chain

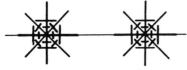

woven spider web

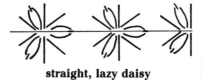

straight, lazy daisy

cross-stitch, straight, French knot

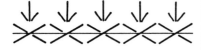

cross-stitch, straight

lazy daisy, straight

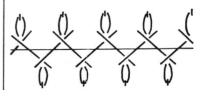

lazy daisy, French knot

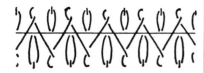

cretan, lazy daisy

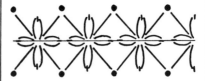

lazy daisy, straight, French knot

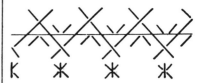

herringbone, cross-stitch, straight

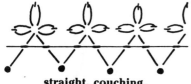

**straight, couching,
lazy daisy, French knot**

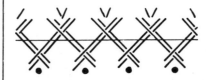

herringbone, straight, French knot

herringbone, lazy daisy

Crochet

CHAIN STITCH: To make first loop on hook, grasp yarn about 2″ from end between left thumb and index finger. With right hand, lap long strand over short end, forming a loop. Hold loop in place with left thumb and index finger. Grasp hook in right hand, insert hook through loop, catch strand with hook and draw it through loop. Pull end and long strand in opposite directions to close loop around hook.

Fig. 1

Figure 1: To make your first chain stitch, pass hook under yarn on index finger and catch strand with hook.

Draw yarn through loop on hook. This makes one chain stitch. Repeat last step until you have as many chains as you need. One loop always remains on hook. Practice making all chains uniform.

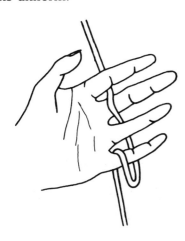

Fig. 2

Figure 2: Weave yarn through left hand.

SINGLE CROCHET:

Fig. 1

Figure 1: Insert hook in second chain from hook. Yarn over hook.

Fig. 2

Figure 2: Draw yarn through chain. Two loops on hook.

Fig. 3

Figure 3: Yarn over hook. Draw yarn through 2 loops on hook. One single crochet has been made.

Fig. 4

Figure 4: Work a single crochet in each chain stitch. At end of row, chain 1 and turn work around.

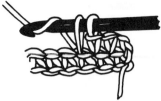

Fig. 5

Figure 5: Insert hook under both top loops of first stitch, yarn over hook and draw through stitch. Yarn over and through 2 loops on hook. Work a single crochet in same way in each stitch across row.

SLIP STITCH: Insert hook in work. Yarn over hook and draw through both the stitch and the loop on hook. Slip stitch makes a firm finishing edge. A single slip stitch is used for joining a chain to form a ring.

Fig. 6

Figure 6: To make a ridge stitch or slipper stitch, work rows of single crochet by inserting hook in back loop only of each single crochet.

HALF DOUBLE CROCHET:

Fig. 1

Figure 1: Yarn over hook. Insert hook in 3rd chain from hook.

HOW TO INCREASE 1 SINGLE CROCHET: Work 2 stitches in 1 stitch.

Fig. 2

Figure 2: Yarn over hook, draw through chain. Yarn over hook again.

HOW TO DECREASE 1 SINGLE CROCHET: Pull up a loop in 1 stitch, pull up a loop in next stitch (3 loops on hook), yarn over hook, draw through all 3 loops at once.

Fig. 3

Figure 3: Draw through all 3 loops on hook. One half double crochet has been made.

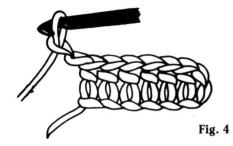

Fig. 4

Figure 4: Work a half double crochet in each chain across. At end of row, ch 2 and turn work.

DOUBLE CROCHET

Fig. 1

Figure 1: Yarn over hook. Insert hook in 4th chain from hook.

Fig. 2

Figure 2: Yarn over hook. Draw through chain. There are 3 loops on hook.

Fig. 3

Figure 3: Yarn over hook. Draw through 2 loops on hook. There are 2 loops on hook. Yarn over hook.

Fig. 4

Figure 4: Draw yarn through remaining 2 loops on hook. One double crochet has been made. When you have worked a double crochet in each chain across, chain 3 and turn work. In most directions, the turning chain 3 counts as first double crochet of next row. In

working the 2nd row, skip the first stitch and work a double crochet in the 2 top loops of each double crochet across. The last double crochet of each row is worked in the top chain of the chain 3 turning chain.

Treble Or Triple Crochet (tr): With 1 loop on hook put yarn over hook twice, insert in 5th chain from hook, pull loop through. Yarn over and draw through 2 loops at a time 3 times. At end of a row, chain 4 and turn. Chain 4 counts as first treble of next row.

Double Treble (dtr): Put yarn over hook 3 times and work off 2 loops at a time as for treble.

Treble Treble (tr tr): Put yarn over hook 4 times and work off 2 loops at a time as for treble.

AFGHAN STITCH

Plain Afghan Stitch: Work with afghan hook. Make a ch desired length.

Row 1: Keeping all lps on hook, sk first ch from hook (lp on hook is first st), pull up a lp in each ch across; Figure 1.

To Work Lps Off: Yo hook, pull through first lp, * yo hook, pull through next 2 lps, repeat from * across until 1 lp remains; Figure 2. Lp that remains on hook always counts as first st of next row.

Row 2: Keeping all lps on hook, sk first vertical bar (lp on hook is first st), pull up a lp under next vertical bar and under each vertical bar across; Figure 3. Work lps off as before. Repeat row 2 for plain afghan stitch.

Edge Stitch: Made at end of rows only to make a firm edge. Work as follows: Insert hook under last vertical bar and in lp at back of bar, pull up 1 lp; Figure 4.

Fig. 1

Fig. 2

Fig. 3

Fig. 4

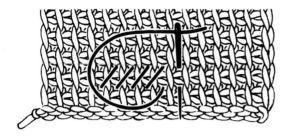

Half Cross-Stitch on Afghan Stitch

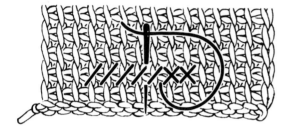

Cross-Stitch on Afghan Stitch

HOW TO TURN YOUR WORK: In crochet a certain number of ch sts are needed at the end of each row to bring work into position for the next row. Then work is turned so reverse side is facing the crocheter. Follow the stitch table below for the number of ch sts to make a turn.

Single crochet (sc)	Ch 1 to turn
Half double crochet (half dc or hdc)	Ch 2 to turn
Double crochet (dc)	Ch 3 to turn
Treble crochet (tr)	Ch 4 to turn
Double treble crochet (dtr)	Ch 5 to turn
Treble treble crochet (tr tr)	Ch 6 to turn

CROCHET ABBREVIATIONS

ch—chain stitch	sc—single crochet
st—stitch	sl st—slip stitch
sts—stitches	dc—double crochet
lp—loop	hdc—half double crochet
inc—increase	tr—treble or triple crochet
dec—decrease	dtr—double treble crochet
rnd—round	tr tr—treble treble crochet
beg—beginning	bl—block
sk—skip	sp—space
p—picot	pat—pattern
tog—together	yo—yarn over hook

MEASURING YOUR GAUGE: Most knitting and crochet directions include a stitch gauge. The stitch gauge gives the number of stitches to the inch with the yarn and hook or needles recommended in the pattern stitch. The directions are based on the given gauge. The gauge (or tension) at which you work controls the size of each finished piece. It is therefore essential to work to the gauge given for each item if you want it to be the correct size. To test your gauge, cast on 20–30 stitches, using the hook or needles specified. Work in the pattern stitches for 3″. Smooth out your swatch and pin it down. Measure across 2″ and place pins 2″ apart. Count number of stitches between pins. If you have more stitches to the inch than directions specify, you are working too tightly; use a larger hook or needles. If you have fewer stitches to the inch, you are working too loosely; use a smaller hook or needles.

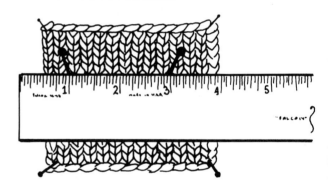

Most patterns give a row gauge, too. Although the proper length does not usually depend on the row gauge (directions usually give lengths in inches rather than rows), in some patterns it is important to have the proper row gauge, too.

HOW TO FOLLOW DIRECTIONS: An asterisk (*) is often used in crochet directions to indicate repetition. For example, when directions read "* 2 dc in next st, 1 dc in next st, repeat from * 4 times" this means to work directions after first * 4 times more. Work 5 times in all.

When parentheses () are used to show repetition, work directions within parentheses as many times as specified. For example, "(dc, ch 1) 3 times" means to do what is within () 3 times altogether.

"Work even" in directions means to work in same stitch without increasing or decreasing.

Knitting

CASTING ON: There are many ways of casting on stitches. The method shown here is only one of them. It gives you a strong and elastic edge.

Fig. 1

Figure 1: Allow enough yarn for the number of stitches to be cast on (about ½" per stitch for lighter weight yarns such as baby yarns, 1" per stitch for heavier yarns such as knitting worsted, more for bulky yarns on large needles). Make a slip loop on needle and tighten knot gently.

Fig. 2

Figure 2: Hold needle in right hand with short end of yarn over left thumb. Weave strand that comes from ball through right hand, over index finger, under second, over third and under fourth finger.

Fig. 3

Figure 3: Bring needle forward to make a loop over left thumb. Insert needle from left to right in loop; bring yarn in right hand under, then over point of needle and draw yarn through loop with tip of needle.

Fig. 4

Figure 4: Keeping right hand in same position, tighten stitch on needle gently with left hand. You now have 2 stitches on needle. Repeat Figures 3 and 4 for required number of stitches.

KNIT STITCH

Fig. 5

Figure 5: Hold needle with cast on stitches in left hand and yarn in same position as for casting on in right hand. Insert point of needle from left to right in first stitch.

Fig. 6

Figure 6: Bring yarn under and over point of right needle.

Fig. 7

Figure 7: Draw yarn through stitch with point of needle.

Fig. 8

Figure 8: Allow loop on left needle to slip off needle. Loop on right needle is your first knit stitch. Repeat from Figure 5 in each loop across row. When you have finished knitting one row, place needle with stitches in left hand ready to start next row.

Garter Stitch: If you work row after row of knit stitch, you are working garter stitch.

PURL STITCH

Fig. 9 Purl

Figure 9: To purl, insert needle from right to left in stitch on left needle. Bring yarn over and under point of right needle: Draw yarn back through stitch and allow loop on left needle to slip off needle.

Stockinette Stitch

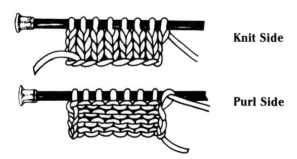

Knit Side

Purl Side

Stockinette Stitch: If you work one row of knit stitch and one row of purl stitch alternately, you are working stockinette stitch.

Reverse Stockinette Stitch If you work one row of purl stitch and one row of knit stitch alternately, you are working reverse stockinette stitch.

BINDING OFF

Fig. 10

Figure 10: Knit the first two stitches. Insert left needle from left to right through front of first stitch. Lift first stitch over second stitch and over tip of right needle. One stitch has been bound off, one stitch remains on right needle. Knit another stitch. Again lift first stitch over second stitch and off right needle. Continue across until all stitches have been bound off. One loop remains on needle. Cut yarn, pull end through loop and tighten knot.

TO INCREASE ONE STITCH: There are several ways to increase a stitch.

Method 1 is illustrated. Knit 1 stitch in the usual way but do not slip it off left needle. Bring right needle behind left needle, insert it from right to left in same stitch (called "the back of the stitch") and make another knit stitch. Slip stitch off left needle. To increase 1 stitch on the purl stitch, purl 1 stitch but do not slip it off left needle. Bring yarn between needles to back, knit 1 stitch in back of same stitch.

Method 2: Pick up horizontal strand between stitch just knitted and next stitch, place it on left needle. Knit 1 stitch in back of this strand, thus twisting it.

Method 3: Place right needle behind left needle. Insert right needle in stitch below next stitch, knit this stitch, then knit stitch above it in the usual way.

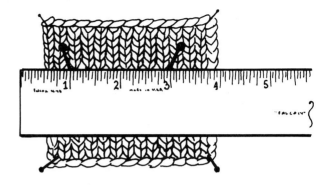

TO DECREASE ONE STITCH: On the right side of work, knit 2 stitches together as in illustration, through the front of the stitches (the decrease slants to the right), or through the back of the stitches (the decrease slants to the left). On the purl side, purl 2 stitches together. Another decrease stitch is called "psso" (pass slip stitch over). When directions say "sl 1, k 1, psso", slip first stitch (take it from left to right needle without knitting it), knit next stitch, then bring slip stitch over knit stitch as in binding off.

KNITTING ABBREVIATIONS	
k—knit	psso—pass slip stitch over
p—purl	inc—increase
st—stitch	dec—decrease
sts—stitches	beg—beginning
yo—yarn over	pat—pattern
sl—slip	lp—loop
sk—skip	MC—main color
tog—together	CC—contrasting color
rnd—round	dp—double-pointed

MEASURING YOUR GAUGE: Most knitting and crochet directions include a stitch gauge. The stitch gauge gives the number of stitches to the inch with the yarn and hook or needles recommended in the pattern stitch. The directions are based on the given gauge. The gauge (or tension) at which you work controls the size of each finished piece. It is therefore essential to work to the gauge given for each item if you want it to be the correct size. To test your gauge, cast on 20–30 stitches, using the hook or needles specified. Work in the pattern stitches for 3″. Smooth out your swatch and pin it down. Measure across 2″ and place pins 2″ apart. Count number of stitches between pins. If you have more stitches to the inch than directions specify, you are working too tightly; use a larger hook or needles. If you have fewer switches to the inch, you are working too loosely; use a smaller hook or needles.

Most patterns give a row gauge, too. Although the proper length does not usually depend on the row gauge (directions usually give lengths in inches rather than rows), in some patterns it is important to have the proper row gauge, too.

HOW TO FOLLOW DIRECTIONS: When parentheses () are used to show repetition, work directions within parentheses as many times as specified. For example, "(K 3, p 2) 5 times" means to do all that is specified in parentheses 5 times in all.

"Place a marker on needle" in directions means to place a safety pin, paperclip, or bought plastic stitch marker on the needle between the stitches. It is slipped from one needle to the other to serve as a mark on following rows.